This book is equally beautiful and challenging. If you want to live life on your heels, soaring by at "average," this message isn't for you. But if you want to rise up, if you want to walk forward in the life Jesus died for you to live, if you want to leave a legacy that will ring out through the ages, *Generation Distinct* will give you the exact tools you need to live life on the offense.

> **LEVI LUSKO,** lead pastor of Fresh Life Church; bestselling author

Having known Hannah Gronowski for years, I can testify that she practices what she writes here. Her words are a clarion call, an anthem, for this generation and the next. If you want your life to mean something, if you hope to impact others, if you believe you were created for more, then step into the *Generation Distinct* journey. To borrow a phrase from Hannah herself, "The question isn't *whether* the world will be changed." The question this book asks is—*Will you be the one to change it?*

> **AUBREY SAMPSON,** author of *The Louder Song*; church planter; speaker

"You're here for a reason." I think we all *want* to believe that, but secretly we might have our doubts. It's why Hannah's book is such a gift to us all. Yes, we live in a world of many wrongs. That's the bad news. The good news is . . . you're here. All you need to do is discover the wrong you're here to make right. Open the book, and find your path.

> **JEFF HENDERSON,** author of *Know What You're FOR*; lead pastor; entrepreneur

Hannah Gronowski is such a refreshing voice! She's deeply biblical, culturally savvy, and one of the finest leaders of our generation. This book is a must-read. It helps unlock the passion, purpose, and potential of one of the most unique generations of all time. If you are ready to dream again, pick this book up NOW.

RASHAWN COPELAND, founder of I'm So Blessed Daily; author of *Start Where You Are*

Hannah Gronowski is one of the key leaders in this next generation. She's a convener, a voice, and a launcher of next-gen leaders. In a generation riddled with stereotypes, I'm thankful for her words on living a distinctly different, set-apart life. She'll help you clarify your calling and move past your excuses.

GRANT SKELDON, executive director of Initiative Network; author of *The Passion Generation*

What if we encouraged and empowered a generation to unleash their God-given gifts and abilities instead of stifling them with criticism and stigmas? In *Generation Distinct*, my friend Hannah Gronowski shows us how Jesus encounters young people and unleashes them to change this world. Be encouraged . . . God is using this generation!

NICK HALL, founder and chief communicator of Pulse

In this work, Hannah shows the world what it means to lead with humility and authority. Her words uplift while they challenge. It's rare to find someone as uniquely gifted for this time as Hannah is.

CARLOS WHITTAKER, author of *Enter Wild*, *Kill the Spider*, and *Moment Maker*

Hannah's passion for living a meaningful life spills all over the pages. She wants that for you, too. This book is not just your invitation but your guide to exploring what's possible for a generation that cares.

CAREY NIEUWHOF, bestselling author; podcaster; speaker

This book is an anthem for this generation! A compelling invitation to live your one and only life with purpose, on mission for the sake of others. Get ready, for these sacred words will call out the best in you and help you live a life that demands an explanation.

STEVE CARTER, pastor; author of *This Invitational Life*

If the future of the next generation is at stake, pass the ball to Hannah. She's the youngest freedom fighter I know. Her book is sure to change lives!

SAM COLLIER, international speaker; global TV and podcast host of *A Greater Story*

At the faith-based university where I'm president, our mission is to help students discover the solution that they were created to be. That is why I am so excited about the impact this book will have on this generation. In *Generation Distinct*, readers will learn how to develop their potential, discover their passions, and connect with their community to multiply their impact.

DR. KENT INGLE, president of Southeastern University; author of *The Modern Guide to College*, *Framework Leadership*, and *9 Disciplines of Enduring Leadership*

GENERATION DISTINCT

GENERATION DISTINCT

DISCOVER THE WRONG YOU
WERE BORN TO MAKE RIGHT

HANNAH GRONOWSKI

A NavPress resource published in alliance
with Tyndale House Publishers

NavPress is the publishing ministry of The Navigators, an international Christian organization and leader in personal spiritual development. NavPress is committed to helping people grow spiritually and enjoy lives of meaning and hope through personal and group resources that are biblically rooted, culturally relevant, and highly practical.

For more information, visit NavPress.com.

Generation Distinct: Discover the Wrong You Were Born to Make Right

Copyright © 2020 by Hannah Gronowski. All rights reserved.

A NavPress resource published in alliance with Tyndale House Publishers

NAVPRESS and the NavPress logo are registered trademarks of NavPress, The Navigators, Colorado Springs, CO. *TYNDALE* is a registered trademark of Tyndale House Ministries. Absence of ® in connection with marks of NavPress or other parties does not indicate an absence of registration of those marks.

The Team:
Don Pape, Publisher; Caitlyn Carlson, Acquisitions Editor; Elizabeth Schroll, Copy Editor; Mark Anthony Lane II, Designer

Cover illustration of marker textures copyright © HEJBRUSH.COM/Creative Market. All rights reserved. Cover photograph of gold texture copyright © Katsumi Murouchi copyright Getty Images. All rights reserved.

Author photograph by Alexandria Bryjak, copyright © 2020. All rights reserved.

Published in association with the literary agent Don Gates of The Gates Group, www.the-gates-group.com.

All Scripture quotations, unless otherwise indicated, are taken from the Holy Bible, *New International Version,*® *NIV.*® Copyright © 1973, 1978, 1984, 2011 by Biblica, Inc.® Used by permission. All rights reserved worldwide. Scripture quotations marked KJV are taken from the *Holy Bible*, King James Version. Scripture quotations marked MSG are taken from *THE MESSAGE*, copyright © 1993, 2002, 2018 by Eugene H. Peterson. Used by permission of NavPress. All rights reserved. Represented by Tyndale House Publishers.

Some of the anecdotal illustrations in this book are true to life and are included with the permission of the persons involved. All other illustrations are composites of real situations, and any resemblance to people living or dead is purely coincidental.

For information about special discounts for bulk purchases, please contact Tyndale House Publishers at csresponse@tyndale.com, or call 1-800-323-9400.

ISBN 978-1-64158-171-4

Printed in the United States of America

26	25	24	23	22	21	20
7	6	5	4	3	2	1

CONTENTS

FOREWORD

I CHUCKLED THE OTHER DAY as I read a recent meme: "Everybody wants to change the world, but no one wants to change the toilet paper!" I laughed so I didn't cry. The stark reality of world-changing conversations is that they are often wildly inspirational without giving much practical help. As G. K. Chesterton wrote, "The Christian ideal has not been tried and found wanting. It has been found difficult; and left untried."[1] This remains true for us, as well, but I'm convinced that the next generation faces an even greater obstacle to applying real-life action to big-picture principles: despair.

There is a fatalistic attitude that lurks as a backdrop to our current cultural thinking. It's no longer just a simple matter of measuring the difficulty of changing the future. It's the overwhelming, seeming pointlessness of change that seeks to defeat us before we even begin. We can find despair in the statistics of next-gen persons who are self-harming, suffering from depression, disconnected from their peers, and considering suicide. Those numbers alone should alarm us. But fatalism is also found in popular theological ideals of comfort and pleasure and wealth and personal blessing that culminate in extreme consumerism and self-growth and personal pleasure in spite of—or maybe as the cause of—global poverty, deep injustices, and racial disparity (to name a few).

What can change this global fatalistic setup, which can only lead us into deeper cycles of oppression both personally (we will drown in our own selfishness) and globally (we will die without change)?

Fire. We need fire. We need to awaken and be lit on fire with a power greater than ourselves and a power that can lead us out of ourselves into the deepest needs of the earth. We need leaders of this era who can speak to the cultural wind of fatalism and command it to be still. We need creative miracle workers who can convince a generation lulled to sleep by a spirit of despair to wake up to their sacred calling and discover their divine worth. We need fire to light up the darkness of the night in order to show us a way forward—to show us that there is light at the end of the tunnel and to send us running in that direction. We need fire that motivates and liberates and sets us all ablaze with hope!

That's why I'm writing the foreword to this book. Hannah is striking a match that can set a generation ablaze. If you read this book, you will not only have some practical ideas of life-changing strategies to help you discover your sacred calling and live it—but you will also have all the flaming energy you need to realize that every time you shine, every time you let your calling and life blaze into the deepest and darkest night (inside or out), you are a beacon of hope that change is possible, that the future can be better, and that things can be different. Maybe our true calling isn't to change the world but to love the world—and to do that, we must start by changing ourselves. This book has that kind of hope woven into its pages.

I'm an eternal optimist. Thousands of years ago, writing to a people figuring out their identity and purpose in the wake of exile, Zechariah called them "prisoners of hope" (Zechariah 9:12). Hannah's voice will help you understand what it is to deal with the stark realities of growing up in this current world—seemingly imprisoned by despair, facing the ideals of a generation who grew up on a steady diet of cynicism ("Whatever") and nihilism ("It doesn't matter") and fatalism ("It won't change"), but who through God's invitation have found something so much better! Hope is an eternal agency of change. And these pages are filled with it. It's not wishful thinking—it's infusing hope into our everyday lives. Our decisions. Our callings. Our gifts. Our impact. It's hope emerging as the source of change, and as Hannah suggests, we fuel this fire together.

As you read these pages, you'll hear the sound of change. It will call you to live differently and equip you to join a people locked into hope as a way of life. This hopeful generation will be distinct, indeed, and will shine like stars on the darkest night. If you think about it, stars are really just cosmic fires, blazing away. As you let your life catch fire, it will blaze and shine hope in this world and light up the darkness. Hannah has convinced me of this—and I pray her words will convince you as well!

Danielle Strickland
Spiritual leader, author, advocate

THE ANTHEM

HERE'S TO YOU.
The wild.
The risky.
The rebels.
The fighters.
The untamed.
The dreamers.
The doers.
The spirited.
The whimsical.
The activists.
The fierce.
The strong.

The bold.
The courageous.

You are my people.
This book is for you.
This book is for us.
This book is for what our world could be if we decide
  to change it.
It won't be easy, and it won't be safe.
But it will be wild. And we like wild.

This is our anthem. This is our rallying cry. This is our
  map. This is our guide.
This is our path into a life that matters. This is our
  conversation about what that even means.
This is about everything your soul has been searching
  for, screaming for, hoping for, yearning for since
  you took your first breath.
This is about what will still matter to you when you
  take your last breath.
This is about life in all of its fullness and beauty and
  magic.
And this is about life in all of its sacrifice and surrender and pain.
This is about adventure and fulfillment and excitement and risk and triumph.
And this is about planting and existing and staying
  where we are.

This book is about passion and purpose and what makes our souls come alive.

And it's about justice and activism and fighting until our last breath to stand up for what is right.

This is about sustainable solutions to devastating injustice.

And this is about everything we must sacrifice if we truly care about justice for all people.

This is about unity and peace and real, authentic, costly love.

This is about linking arms, reaching across divides, and inviting more voices to the table.

This is about a Jesus I have encountered who is better, more beautiful, more radical, more untame, more risky, more wild than I ever imagined.

This is about living a life that matters.

This is your story, and this is mine.

Let's go on a wild adventure together.

Let's live lives that matter.

INTRODUCTION

YOU WANT TO LIVE A LIFE THAT MATTERS. You want to fight for change. You want to create beauty. You want to unleash hope. You want to advocate for justice. You want to live a bigger story. You want to build a better future.

I know because, well, me too. I'm just like you.

I'm Hannah. I'm twenty-five. I was born with a neon soul and freedom in my lungs. A lust for life is both my edge and my curse. I believe in hope. I believe in unity. People are my lifeblood. I think we're stronger together. I believe every voice matters. Even mine. Even yours. And I think every person should have a place at the table.

I believe in justice. I believe in equality. I believe your

story and perspective is important and should be heard. I believe in a love that crosses divides and breaks the rules and honors each and every life. I think love is truly the most powerful force for change.

I'm a human. I'm a friend. I'm a sister. I'm a leader. I'm a dreamer. I'm a doer. I'm a little bit wild, with a wanderer's soul. And I am never more at home than when I'm somewhere I've never been.

I know life is meant to be lived in all of its magnitude. I am confident our stories can be written to change the course of history. I am convinced ordinary people have the potential to create extraordinary impact.

I'm tired of the old ways of living. I'm over the ordinary. I'm bored of the bland. And I hate being reduced to the label *religious*. I follow Jesus. Not because I have to. But because I want to. Because I have encountered a Jesus who embodies a wildly unprecedented brand of love.

And . . . I really want to live a life that matters. I want to leave a mark on this world. I want my impact to echo throughout eternity. I want to empower people and build things that last and do something about the pain I see around me. I want to create. I want to change. I want to advocate. I want to march. I want to influence. I want to invest. I want to liberate. I want to lead.

This book is full of stories and ideas and questions

and doubts and invitations and opportunities and dreams and truths. These are the records of my journey as I have embarked on a quest to discover how to live a life that matters. And this is your invitation to begin a journey of your own into a whole new kind of life.

Life is beautiful. But it's also sacred. And when we live into the paradox of the beautifully sacred gift of life, we learn to thrive. As you flip through these pages, I won't tell you how to live. Instead, I just want to share what I've learned. Because through a winding journey of mistakes and victories and laughter and tears, I've discovered something I always hoped was possible but wasn't sure I could find.

I didn't find a perfect life. I didn't find an easy life. I didn't find a glamorous life. But I found a life that really matters. And that is the very best kind of life.

Here we go. The time is now. Let's go on a wild adventure together to discover what it really means to live a life that matters.

THE LIE OF COMFORT

I'm nineteen years old, and I'm choking on my comfort. The very thing I thought would bring me freedom is tying me down tighter every day. I've chased comfort as though it's the goal of my life. But every time I think I succeed, the comfort seems to slip right through my tightly locked fingers—coaxing me even further into its deceit. Comfort promises a life that is good and predictable and orderly. It promises a good life that will make you . . . *happy*. It promises you'll stay safe and be successful and life will finally be . . . easy. But really, I'm just trying to be someone who looks good on paper. And I feel like a shadow of who I'm created to be.

My soul is tired of pretending. I want to live a life that matters. But I'm not even sure what that means.

I'm looking for a life that is adventurous and wild and full and exciting. I used to dream and plan and create goals and write bucket lists. I thought by this point of my life, I would have built five schools in developing countries and backpacked across Europe and rescued girls off the street in Thailand and rock climbed in Yosemite and empowered every homeless family in downtown Chicago.

But instead, I find myself lying in bed, my alarm clock blaring, the freezing winter air shoving me back under the covers. Eventually, I get up, take a shower, and grab the lunch I packed for the day. My car doesn't start because it's older than I am, and I fumble nervously with the jumper cables. Finally, I am on my way, texting frantically at a stoplight to let the team know I'm running late. Overwhelmed and discouraged, I get to the office and throw my stuff down on my desk as I hustle to the meeting and collapse in a chair at a large round table.

I try hard to focus on the meeting, but the daily narrative once again plays on a loop in my head: *I want to live a life that matters. But this isn't it.*

Someone calls on me, and I am dragged back into reality. I quiet my soul. I tell her to behave. I tell her to stop. I don't want to hear those thoughts anymore. They're not practical. They're not attainable. My soul is exhausted as she boldly competes with the rush, the hurry, the loud pace of my life. My soul was once bright, neon, wild—and now she seems to have retreated so deeply within me, I can barely hear her tired voice pleading for a chance to come alive again. I know something needs to change.

I have heard whispers of the kind of life I wanted to live. I've seen glimpses of a different type of existence. I've read stories full of wild meaning; I just don't know how to write my own. If I am ever going to live a life that matters, I know everything needs to change.

Later that night, I sit in a room full of young adults on a bone-chilling February Chicago night, and I hear the same longing—the soundtrack of my generation. Not like my favorite soundtrack that I'd pop in for a weekend road trip—more like the broken record player you'd find at a great-aunt's house that plays the same shrill melody over and over and over. Everyone is annoyed by it, but no one tries to fix it.

We are dripping with dreams. We feel the rumblings of more, knowing the world is broken and wanting to have a part in making it right. And on this dreary winter night, I look around and know that every person in this room is packed with potential. Each of us longs, aches, for all that life *could* be.

But something holds us back. I shift awkwardly in my seat. It feels like someone has sucked the oxygen out of the room. We desperately yearn for a life full of deep relationships and loud laughter and authentic faith, of thrilling adventure and world-changing risk and wide-eyed wonder. But the dreary conversation settles, instead, on why that life is just too far out of reach for our normal, ordinary existence. Work is *hard*. Life is *rough*. Relationships are *difficult*. Responsibility feels *stifling*. We drearily ponder what to do with our lives.

We have become discouraged, tame, quiet, unsure. Our vision and potential and passions and dreams are sitting off in a corner collecting dust, their colors fading with each passing day. Resignation has seeped into our everyday lives, convincing us the impossible we once dreamed of was just that: impossible.

And one by one, we are missing the story we were created to write.

A WHOLE NEW WAY TO LIVE

I think God had me in mind when He created mountains.

When I first saw the Rockies from the plane window on my first trip to Colorado, my heart did a backflip, and the smile on my face didn't budge at any point over the next five days. Something about being surrounded by mountains makes me feel small and strong all at once. I love that about our God—that He created us with the instinct to love and admire His handiwork. I love that He connected our hearts to different elements of what He has created. I just think that was so cool of Him.

My friend Faith and I arrived in Colorado Springs with very little agenda. We were there for adventure. We had booked a ticket for the Centennial State in a moment of adventurous impulse, found friends who would generously share their house with us, and boarded a plane with high hopes and mountainous visions.

Once we arrived, we asked everyone we met what our "must dos" should be during our five days in the Springs. We decided to spend our days exploring the Garden of the Gods and rock climbing at Red Rock Canyon and finding the best coffee shops in town.

But one morning, we were greeted by rain softly pattering on the roof and heavy fog swirling outside our window. For a while, we wandered aimlessly around the house. We were listless, our adrenaline still hanging thick in the air as our eyes drifted over the unfinished list of planned activities. Reluctantly, we admitted we would have to wait out the rain.

We weren't sure what to do next. We wandered into the front room and peered out the rain-striped window—and noticed a dry wooden swing under a covering, swaying gently in the rainstorm.

We grabbed pillows and blankets and hot cups of coffee and hurried out to the swing. And there we sat for the next three hours, the mist from the rain gently brushing our faces as we looked out toward the fog-draped mountains. We pulled the blankets just a little bit tighter. There we sat, reflecting fondly on the many magical moments we had experienced that week.

Something about sitting on that swing amid the gloom and the misty mountains felt sacred. We spoke in hushed tones, hesitant to disrupt the weight of the moment.

The moments spent on that swing changed the direction of my life. We talked about our longings to devote our lives to something greater than ourselves. We admitted the thirst within our souls to sacrifice deeply to create real change in our world. We gently whispered the dissatisfaction we felt in our relatively comfortable lives. We yearned to stop just talking about injustice and start doing something about it. We wrestled with big ideas and scary dreams together. We refused to apologize for a belief we held that God could use us—yes, even us—to mark history in a profound way.

We dreamed bold dreams about what it would look like to start . . . *something*. Something that would provide an anthem for a tribe of tenacious, passionate, wild young leaders—calling them to abolish cultural complacency, unleash lasting justice, and join an adventure following our untamable God. It's what our souls were hungry for. And we believed it was what our generation around the world was hungry for as well.

I looked up at the tips of the Rockies, just visible above the fog, and wondered aloud, "What if we're talking about discovering *a whole new way to live*?"

It was as though, just for a moment, heaven touched earth. Something sacred was taking place on that little wooden swing on a rainy day in Colorado.

Faith smiled. "Yes, Hannah. Let's discover a whole new way to live."

A LIFE THAT MATTERS

The most monumental moments of history can often be traced back to a small, passionate band of brothers and sisters who refused to allow the world to stay as it was. These radical individuals were driven by a vision of the future so compelling, they were willing to sacrifice everything they had and all they were to see the world changed. They linked arms. They claimed their cause. They rose up. And they have marked our

GENERATION DISTINCT

"THE MOST MONUMENTAL MOMENTS OF HISTORY CAN OFTEN BE TRACED BACK TO A SMALL, PASSIONATE BAND OF BROTHERS AND SISTERS WHO REFUSED TO ALLOW THE WORLD TO STAY AS IT WAS."

history books. They have changed our realities. They have altered our world forever.

The apostle Peter and his band of disciples traveled all around the known world to spread the movement of the early church. William Wilberforce led the Clapham Sect and forever transformed the culture in England. George Washington and his unlikely army defeated the powerhouse of the day to start a new country characterized by freedom. Martin Luther King Jr. and his team of friends and allies rallied together in the pursuit of equality and justice.

I believe you and I stand at a crossroads in history. Our world is desperately calling out to the next band of passionate, gritty, tenacious young leaders, asking them to rise up and demand a different type of world.

A world of hope. A world of unity. A world of beauty and honor and a pure kind of love. A world of justice and truth, where we stand together instead of tearing each other apart. A world of equality. A world of opportunity. A world where every single life matters.

And perhaps . . . *we* are the leaders, the next band of brothers and sisters, who will leave a mark on history.

The question isn't *whether* the world will be changed. The question is, Who will change it?

When God was laying out the strategy for the

entire world, He wrote your name down on this day, in your place, with your passions, for a reason. I don't know exactly what it looked like for God to create this grand strategy. But I like to imagine what it could have been like.

I imagine: Before the first flash of light ever comes into existence, Father, Spirit, and Son are sitting together at a table. Next to the table is a large white-board, too big to even describe. And the Spirit begins to say the names, one by one, of the people who will one day inhabit the earth God is about to create:

"Maria."

"Muhammad."

"Jose."

"Anna."

"Oscar."

"Sasha."

"Jamena."

"Adrienne."

As the Father hears each name, a fond smile spreads across His face as He thinks about one of that person's funny quirks, or a sweet story from their childhood, or a magical moment they'll encounter as an adult. He turns around and writes that name in bold ink on the whiteboard, with arrows and dotted lines and circles connecting each person into the grand story He is weaving. As He writes each name, the web grows thicker, and each name becomes more and more essential. A name is no longer just a name. It is a person who will influence another person, who will influence another person, who will influence another person. It goes on and on and on.

Eventually, He says my name. God laughs, knowing the crazy and wild soul He will place within me and my loud laugh He knows will startle people in coffee shops, and the love He will give me for mountains and deserts and oceans and forests.

He shakes His head lovingly, knowing I will desperately search for adventure and get myself into all sorts of trouble along the way. He knows the ache and longing that will rise up within me to see wrong things made right in our world. And then, He turns around and writes my name on the board. My name is surrounded by the people who have impacted my life: my mentors, my pastors, my family, my friends, and the countless leaders who have loved me, led me, and invested in me.

Rippling out from my name are the high school girls I mentor, and the refugee kids I get to hang out with, and the baristas at my favorite coffee shop, and the Generation Distinct Tribe, and the staff I lead, and maybe even some people I will never even meet. Maybe even your name is there. Names upon names, woven together and interconnected.

Finally, the Spirit says, "That's all of our children."

Father, Son, and Spirit take a step back and look

lovingly at this whiteboard full of names. A masterpiece of people. A web of impact. A mosaic of lives and talents and places and passions and dreams and callings and encounters and stories. The Father's gaze falls on Jesus, and He whispers, "This is all possible because of the rescue plan, because we love each and every one of these people enough to risk it all, to sacrifice everything to redeem them."

Then, with the air full of expectancy, God loudly proclaims, "Let there be light." And the world begins.

Who has your life touched? What injustice could be crossed off because your name comes onto the scene? What names will never ripple outward unless your name first connects with them?

You are not an extra name, a last-minute addition, or a forgotten element. You have an essential, pivotal role in God's strategy for the redemption and restoration of this world. Do not miss it. Do not waste your life wondering when someone will finally invite you to participate. Because the very moment God placed you on this earth, He was issuing you and me an invitation to *life*.

You're *invited* to love without hindrance.
You're *invited* to live with great intentionality.
You're *invited* to laugh as loud as you'd like.
You're *invited* to lead with remarkable courage.
You're *invited* to travel far and wide.

"YOU HAVE AN ESSENTIAL, PIVOTAL ROLE IN GOD'S STRATEGY FOR THE REDEMPTION AND RESTORATION OF THIS WORLD."

You're *invited* to stay home and invest in the people you love.

You're *invited* to create beautiful art.

You're *invited* to fight for justice around the world.

You're *invited* to confront the injustice in your own hometown.

You're *invited* to make great speeches.

You're *invited* to dress in bright colors.

You're *invited* to speak boldly for truth.

You're *invited* to preach the gospel on a stage.

You're *invited* to preach the gospel in back alleys.

You're *invited* to create relationships across divides of race and culture.

You're *invited* to start world-changing initiatives.

You're *invited* to provide a meal for a hungry man in your city.

You're *invited* to welcome people into your home.

You're *invited* to design beautiful spaces for community to happen.

You're *invited* to write soulful poetry.

You're *invited* to start groundbreaking companies.

You're *invited* to raise funds for children across the globe.

You're *invited* to pour into the lives of children in your own neighborhood.

You're *invited*.

What are you waiting for? Don't waste your life waiting for an *invitation* you have already received. God is still calling to His people and asking, "Whom shall I send? And who will go for us?" He doesn't force us to say yes. He *invites*. He asks. And He waits for us to respond and say, "Here am I. Send me!" (Isaiah 6:8).

The *invitation* is already extended. Let's be a generation that raises our hands, jumping up and down, waving our arms, calling out God's name, and yelling, "Send me. Send me. *Send me!*" You're *invited* into this wild adventure of life.

Jesus wants to thrill us. To invite us into a life so risky and wild and unsafe that we finally discover what we were created for. He wants to make our eyes wide with wonder and our souls fully alive. And He is reaching out His hand, whispering to us about the wild adventures that await us if we will only say yes. Adventures that are sometimes difficult and painful, that require great amounts of sacrifice. And yet. These adventures will fulfill our deepest longings for meaning, our soulful search for fulfillment, and our great grasp for purpose. These adventures are what we were created for.

Right now, I find myself sitting on the very same porch swing I sat on a few years ago as my friend and I dreamed of embarking on a journey to discover a whole new way of living. And do you know what we discovered? This. This book is the chronicle of what we discovered. These chapters are the narratives of my past few years, which I've spent exploring and discovering a brand-new kind of life. This new life didn't move me across the globe or make me sell all my possessions or take me backpacking to find myself or lead me to an orphanage in another country. Because this journey is not about taking you *out* of your life. It's about discovering the purpose and passions and dreams that have always been right there in your life, waiting for you to look them in the eyes and simply say yes.

I am blown away at the path Jesus led me along. These chapters are not a random assortment of some good ideas or helpful suggestions. They are simply the guideposts that continued to push me forward on my own journey into discovering a life that really matters—and maybe, along the way, you'll be able to find the markers for your own journey.

We don't need a list of rules. We're over that. We need an anthem that will rally a generation to action.

MOVEMENT #1: OWN YOUR POTENTIAL

Nothing will change if we don't believe, beyond the shadow of a doubt, that change is possible and that it starts with us. Our anthem will begin as we claim the potential we have to lead our world into a new future.

GENERATION DISTINCT MOVEMENTS

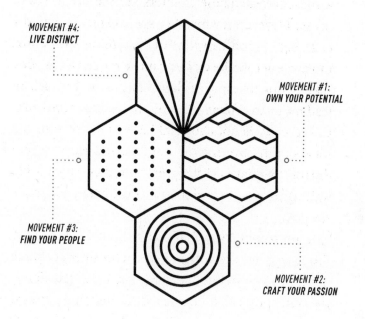

MOVEMENT #4:
LIVE DISTINCT

MOVEMENT #1:
OWN YOUR POTENTIAL

MOVEMENT #3:
FIND YOUR PEOPLE

MOVEMENT #2:
CRAFT YOUR PASSION

MOVEMENT #2: CRAFT YOUR PASSION

If we want to see our world transformed, we need a generation of leaders who are living out their passions with great conviction, deep commitment, and untamable vision. Our anthem will declare our devotion to crafting our passions from the inside out—taking an honest look at what justice really means and embarking with purpose and strategy to actually transform our world.

MOVEMENT #3: FIND YOUR PEOPLE

Reshaping our world is impossible in the absence of unity. To witness justice unleashed, hope spread, and love rule, we'll need to reach across divides, link arms in unity, and charge together into a whole new future. Our anthem will give words to the stirrings of our soul for love to overcome hate and unity to sweep across our world.

MOVEMENT #4: LIVE DISTINCT

This vision is not just about us. It is about what the world *could* be if we decide to change it. It is about what lies ahead. Together, we can trailblaze a whole new way of living for the individuals yet to be born. This anthem will set our sights on the future as we create a brand-new way of living not just for ourselves but also for those who come after us.

This book isn't just a book. It's an invitation into a whole new life.

The future generations depend on us to break the chains and blaze the trail.

The world is waiting.

So, friends, don't wait to begin your own journey into a whole new way to live. Don't put it off until tomorrow. Don't convince yourself that a better time or an easier season of life will come along. *This* is your porch swing moment.

And maybe, in three years, you'll find yourself once again sitting on your own "porch swing," and you will shake your head in wonder as you reflect on the journey Jesus has led you on, and you, too, will be able to say with deep conviction, "I am truly living a life that matters."

It's time to stand up, shake off the fear, embrace the unknown, and run into this adventure. It's time to refuse to stay safe, to settle into mundane routine, to keep life easy, or to remain complacent. Instead, let's link arms together as we storm the gates of this world with truth and love and honor and justice and light.

Let's lead the way for our world. Let's become the leaders of change, of justice, and of redemption. It's time for you and me to rise.

Our world is ready to realize a radical new way to live. A life that is deeper and wilder. A life full of purpose and passion and impact. A life of risk and heart-pumping excitement. A life lived alongside a tribe of people. A life of building things that last. A life of creating beauty that brings change. A life of grander stories. A life of fulfillment. A life that creates a whole new world for the generations to come. A life that really matters.

A spark has been lit in the souls of our tribe. Us. This generation. The young leaders. And it will spread like wildfire as we pass it on to the generations surrounding us. This movement will begin as ordinary people live their rebuttal to the stereotype of our generation as apathetic.

This won't happen by accident. It will happen as we take real action, together, to remake our lives, remake our communities, remake our countries, remake our world.

Are you ready?

Your wild adventure is about to begin.

Let's live lives that really matter.

MOVEMENT #1

OWN YOUR POTENTIAL

Unlikely Leaders

THE SUN GLISTENS OFF THE OCEAN in front of me like light glistens off soft, plush velvet. The waves are gently embracing the shore where I'm sitting, while white seabirds circle overhead, their color contrasting poetically against the intense blue of the morning sky. The whole world feels still and peaceful, wrapping me in mauve as the sun peeks over the horizon.

And I wonder if the Sea of Galilee might have looked a little bit like this as Peter and Andrew dragged their boats back into the water for another day of doing exactly what they did every other day. Rowing. Casting. Catching. Hauling. Cleaning. Selling.

There is something so paradoxical about routine. Most of us claim to hate monotony in principle. If I asked you, "Do you want to live a monotonous life?" you would probably say no. Who wants to live a life of settling for the same thing, over and over? But really, we are often addicted to the safety, the knowability of routine.

Your life might be more monotonous than you even realize. You want your life to make lasting impact. But as you look at your calendar, you wonder if anything you did over the past week actually . . . *mattered*.

Because the opposite of monotony is not excitement. The opposite of monotony is meaning.

I imagine life felt monotonous for Peter and Andrew as they dragged their boat back into the water day after day, wiping the sweat off their foreheads and looking out at the condition of the sea. This was what they did every day. It was their normal. It was their safe. It was their ordinary. In many ways, it was exactly what their culture *expected* of them. They weren't given the opportunity to continue their formal education. So . . . they became fishermen. And there they sat. Minding their own business, sweating in the heat of the day, dirty from a long day of work, ordinary and overlooked in every way.

Most theologians and people who are way smarter than I am agree that at the time when we meet these unlikely heroes in the book of Matthew (Matthew

4:18-22), Peter was in his early twenties and Andrew was in his late teens. These were no prophetic leaders. They weren't brilliant orators. They weren't wealthy business owners. They were just Peter and Andrew, two young guys who caught fish.

And right in the center of the normalcy of their lives, Jesus walks onto the scene.

I don't know what you think about Jesus. But you don't have to believe what I believe to learn something from the life of this world-altering individual. Jesus Christ wasn't just some nice man who talked about morals. His life launched the greatest movement of all time. His name is known around the globe. His teachings are proclaimed to millions of people every day. People of nearly every language and nation and race worship Him. Individuals of all socioeconomic classes follow Him and study His life. He was a rebel with a cause worth fighting for. He was a revolutionary whose followers shook up the world. He was a leader who turned the religious systems upside down.

I believe Jesus is the God of the world, the Creator of the universe, and the Savior of all humanity. But whatever you do or don't believe about Jesus at this point, we can all agree on one thing: We have something to learn from the most influential person in all of history.

This guy, Jesus, was on a mission to save the entire

human race and launch a worldwide movement that would alter the rest of history. And you would think, at this point of the story when He meets Peter and Andrew, Jesus would be in all-out recruitment mode. For a mission as grand and important as His, we'd expect Him to be searching for the brightest minds, the most eloquent communicators, the most experienced leaders. Surely He'd head for the Temple to track down the religious leaders or toward the palace to recruit the royalty. Because change always happens out of the centers of power, from the smart and the privileged, right?

But maybe Jesus sees the world differently than we do. Because on that normal day in Galilee, Jesus walked toward the boats. As He scanned the crowd, His gaze fell on two dirty young faces. And I imagine He smiled. These two fishermen had no idea their entire lives were about to change forever.

> As Jesus was walking beside the Sea of Galilee, he saw two brothers, Simon called Peter and his brother Andrew. They were casting a net into the lake, for they were fishermen. *"Come, follow me,"* Jesus said, "and I will send you out to fish for people." At once they left their nets and followed him.
>
> MATTHEW 4:18-20, AUTHOR'S EMPHASIS

Later in the story, we learn that God chose Peter to be the rock of His church. Jesus looked straight in the eyes of this scruffy, loudmouthed, uncensored, passionate young man and said, "On *you*, I will build my church" (Matthew 16:18, author's paraphrase).

In other words, "Peter—I am going to start a movement. This movement is going to change all of history and all of eternity. This movement must spread to all corners of the world, and it must impact people who will be born thousands and thousands of years from now. And it is all going to happen under your leadership. You. The uneducated, foot-in-your-mouth, twentysomething guy. *You* will lead this movement."

Jesus could have chosen someone important. He could have chosen someone polished. He very well could have chosen someone who was older or more experienced or more qualified. But Jesus just didn't. And I love that He didn't.

Everything changed for Peter and Andrew that day on the lake. They were drawn out of their mediocrity and invited into meaning. They were called out of ordinary and given the gift of extraordinary. They were shaken out of normal and drawn into a radical new way of life. Because someone showed up who was powerful enough, radical enough, just crazy enough to see the potential in those two ordinary kids. And I know this about Jesus: He sees the potential in you, too.

Sometimes, we can hear the stories of how this whole idea of Christianity came to be and we picture it all starting with old men in thick robes drearily pondering deep thoughts about God. My view of Jesus changed forever when I began to understand who it was He invited to be the original members of His world-changing team.

I don't think Jesus approached Peter because there was no one else at the docks that day, or because He couldn't find the Temple, or because the royal family turned Him down. I think Jesus was making a statement about young people for the rest of history. I think Jesus was creating a new precedent for the people the world calls "unqualified." Because when Jesus sees the young, unlikely, unqualified people in our world, He doesn't dismiss them. He doesn't scold them for their questions or their struggles or their fears. He doesn't see apathy, and He doesn't see the problems in our society. Rather, He sees a group of people He can use to shake up the world and to start a movement.

How can it be that Jesus sees the world so differently? How can it be that Jesus chose the unlikely in our world? How can it be that Jesus started the most influential movement of all time with a team of ragtag teens and twentysomethings? What would compel Him to show up at the shore and disrupt the normal lives of two so-called ordinary young men? What kind of love would compel Him to see past what the world sees to uncover the people He knew they *could* be?

HOW ABOUT YOU?

I was a sixteen-year-old who wanted to change things. I wanted justice to be unleashed through my little life. My young soul wanted to advocate for people and rescue the oppressed and change the world in every grand way. But . . . I didn't have any clue where to begin. I remember spending months with the question spinning around in my mind, *How can I change the world?*

I pleaded with Jesus to show me what I was created for. I wanted to know what it would look like—really look like—to live for something larger than myself.

One quiet Saturday afternoon I walked through the aisles of a used bookstore, my fingers brushing gently across the faded, worn book spines. I was sure they held the secrets of life within their yellowed pages. And I was searching for answers, desperate for direction. I stumbled on a book that dripped with promise and brought it home to crack open its wisdom. I sat on the couch and, as I peered into the pages, I felt like everything was about to change.

I read story after story of the injustice infiltrating our world. And as I read each sentence of the book, my heart broke just a little deeper.

Starvation, slavery, homelessness, trafficking, racism, violence, poverty, and more and more and more. The pain of the world felt heavy on my sixteen-year-old shoulders. As I closed the book after reading it in one sitting, I couldn't find words. I didn't know what to do with this burden I held in my hands.

But in that moment, the God of the universe chose to place a vision in the heart of an unlikely teenager—one I will never forget. I felt Him tell me, "Hannah, you are not called to solve all of the injustice in the world yourself. But I want to use you to empower your generation to fight against the injustice in this world."

The vision was intoxicating. Something woke up within me. I ran up to my bedroom, dug out a white-board, and furiously drew out plans and ideas and visions for what it could look like to truly empower my generation. How could we, together, discover the wrong we were born to make right? What if our generation could be the answer to the world's greatest needs?

And then, a few years later, I found myself in that soul-draining routine. I was more discouraged, more confused, more burdened than ever. So many in my generation were settling for mediocre stories. We were entrenched in the expectations of the world, controlled by the culture's push for more, marked by a lack of meaning, desperate for a different kind of life. My generation was sprinting from the church, convinced that the excitement, adventure, and risk they were searching for certainly would never be found within the four walls of religion.

I didn't know what to do. So I started to talk to God about it.

"God," I whispered, "somebody has to tell my generation we don't need to walk away from you in order to find the life we are searching for. Somebody has to tell my generation we have so much potential. Somebody has to tell my generation we don't need to wait until we are older or until we have our life figured out to start creating real impact in our world."

And in that moment, I sensed God whisper back, "That's right, Hannah. How about *you*?"

Those three words have the potential to change everything about our lives. Or nothing about our lives. It's up to us. We can say yes. We can say no. We can raise our hands, or we can back away slowly. We can take action, or we can stay right where we're at.

But God offers us the courage to say yes, if we're willing.

I said yes. I was completely terrified, utterly unsure, and absolutely exhilarated. When Faith and I got home from our trip in Colorado, we shared the vision with a few close friends. Together, we began to dream and plan and create and build a path into a better kind of future. We spent hours in coffee shops, asking big questions. We stayed up late and woke up early to dream about what *could be*. We wondered, *How can we empower our generation to live lives that really matter?*

Before we were ready, we just started making things. We built a website and gathered more people and shot some videos and created curriculum. Before we knew it, a mobilizing organization called Generation Distinct was born.

Today, my friends and I still laugh at the wide-eyed, naive people we were five years ago when this journey began. We were just crazy enough, just hopeful enough to believe we could change the world. And that is exactly what we set out to do.

I now find myself living a more wild, risky, beautiful life than I could ever have imagined—not because my life is glamorous or perfect. Because it's not. It's entirely imperfect, often messy, somewhat wild, and always unknown. Some days I want to quit. I want to find something easier, less risky, not quite so big. But at the end of my life, I don't think I'll wish I had spent my days doing anything else. Because I get to wake up every day knowing that I am truly living a life that matters.

Every day, I get to empower young leaders around the globe to discover how they, too, can live lives that matter. Together we are discovering the wrongs we were born to make right and experiencing more beautiful, free, fulfilling lives than ever before. Ultimately,

I get to lead people to experience who Jesus Christ really is. And that is the most important work I could ever do. Lives are being changed, and greater stories are being written.

But here's the thing: This isn't happening because I am brilliant or smart or qualified for this calling. In all honesty, I'm not. Most days I still don't think I'm the one for the job. Sometimes, it can feel like the hate in our world is too deep, the injustice too fierce, the pain too prevalent, the terror too heavy. Who am I to do something about it? Who am I to use my voice? Who am I to think my one life can make any sort of difference? What say should I have in creating change in the world? What do I really bring to the table? I'm not the best leader or the most creative innovator. I'm not the most well-educated about injustice or the most qualified person for the job. I'm not really old enough or experienced enough. I often feel weak and afraid. I usually feel in over my head. I question why God would see any sort of potential in me. But He does.

You see, my opportunities don't *qualify* me. The zip code I was born into doesn't *qualify* me. The advantages I have received don't *qualify* me.

And my limitations don't *disqualify* me. My age doesn't *disqualify* me. My lack of a business degree doesn't *disqualify* me. My limited life experience doesn't *disqualify* me.

Maybe you feel you were given more opportunities

than limitations. If that's you, what are you *doing* with the opportunities and advantages you have been given? Because to whom much is given, much is required (see Luke 12:48). Your opportunities aren't an excuse to sit back and get comfortable. Rather, you have a responsibility to *steward* those opportunities to fight for the futures of others.

Maybe you feel you were given more limitations than opportunities. If that's you, then you're in good company. All throughout history we see God use the most unlikely, overlooked, forgotten, unknown people to change the world. Your limitations aren't an excuse to opt out of God's calling on your life. Because what society deems as limitations are really opportunities for God to show off His power.

Here's the truth: Only the One who created us has the right and ability to qualify us for our calling. And the good news is, God doesn't see us the way the world sees us. He doesn't see us for who we currently are. He sees us for who we could be. He sees us for our potential. Because He created us, after all. He knows all that lies within us. He placed within us skills and abilities that are waiting to be uncovered. We don't uncover them and *then* use them; we uncover them *as* we use them. When we are pushed out of what's comfortable, to the edge of where we think we can go, suddenly we discover how God equips us to go even further.

Nothing can disqualify us from the calling God has placed on our lives. If He has called us, He will qualify us. If He has invited us, He will equip us. If He has sent us, He will give us everything we need to say yes.

I so want you to experience the Jesus I have met. I so want you to meet the most radical individual to ever have stepped foot on this planet. I am so hungry for you to encounter this Jesus who wants to lead you into a more adventurously expectant life than you ever could imagine. Please. *Please.* Don't miss the most incredible invitation ever given. It's right here, and it's extended to you. Jesus is reaching out, inviting you into a whole new, radical, wild way of living with the same three words He has been using all along to gather revolutionaries together and shake up the world: "Come, follow Me."

The only question is, how are you going to respond?

BREAK THE RULES

A couple of months ago, some friends offered to lend me their 1997 Jeep Wrangler for a week while they were out of town.

I took them up on their offer in a snap and assured them I would take great care of it. The next morning, a few friends and I loaded up beach chairs, an Igloo cooler, and brightly colored towels into our borrowed vehicle and set off for the hour-long drive to the Lake Michigan beachfront.

When we finally arrived, our mouths were dry from singing loudly to the radio, and our skin was raw from the wind whipping across our faces. We unloaded our beach gear, walked down to the shore, and situated ourselves on the beach, feet in the water and books on our laps.

Everything was perfect. The sun was warm. The sand was soft. The lap of the waves was steady and soothing. For a brief fifteen minutes, everything was exactly right.

And then I felt a thick raindrop land on my forehead. I huddled under an umbrella and watched the fog grow thicker over the water and the rain turn the soft sand a deeper shade of brown. I was staying put.

But as the thunder and lightning grew louder and brighter, my friends gently suggested I was being ridiculous. I finally relented and we surrendered our spot on the shore to begin the journey back up the beach.

We ran, rain spitting in our faces and chairs slipping out of our grasps—and then we paused abruptly and looked at each other. Someone yelled, "Our car has no . . . roof!"

The rain had become a heavy, intense downpour. We hobbled with our beach chairs, umbrellas, towels, and cooler toward the nearest shelter we could find. We eventually found an overhang where other people with wet bathing suits and discouraged expressions sat staring at the steady deluge coming from the dark sky.

We waited there . . . for hours. We sat, we talked, we ate cherries from our cooler. We made conversation with our new friends as we united around our common dilemma. We watched as person after person mustered enough courage to run to their cozy, safe cars. But our car had no roof or doors. So we waited, and waited, and waited.

Eventually, the park maintenance crew came by to inform us they were closing the park for the night. We had no choice but to brave the storm and hope beyond all hope we would make it home in one piece. So we ran for it, up the hill and back toward the street where the now-lonely Jeep still stood like a brave lone soldier who had refused to retreat. We awkwardly threw our beach gear in the back, wrapped ourselves in garbage bags and towels, and began to drive.

The rain continued, and the wind whipped around us. The thunder boomed and the lightning flashed. The storm raged on. But I was laughing loud, my eyes wide with wonder. I had never ridden in an open Jeep during a rainstorm. Maybe you have, but I hadn't. And let me tell you . . . people noticed us.

The Jeep was so full of water that, at stoplights,

we had to take out Styrofoam bowls and start bailing water out of the bottom of our vehicle. Other cars' passengers rolled down their windows to cheer us on, laughing with us (or at us—I'm still not sure). When we were twenty minutes away from home, the rain began to pour even harder. Moms in minivans stared at us in horror, and high schoolers in small beaters stared at us in envy.

We were making quite the scene, and every other car's occupants were watching us.

Maybe it was because we were out in an open Jeep in the pouring rain. Or maybe it was because we looked strange, all wrapped up in towels and garbage bags. Or, just maybe, it was because they saw the wonder on our faces. Maybe they could hear my laughter above the thunder and they could see the whimsy in my eyes. They could tell I was living a moment I would never forget, and, maybe, they wished they had more moments like that in their own lives.

We were rule breakers that day. We "shouldn't" have driven an open Jeep in the middle of a severe thunderstorm. But we did, and others noticed.

Maybe we *shouldn't* change the world. Maybe we *shouldn't* battle against oppression. Maybe we *shouldn't* rescue people out of exploitation. Maybe we *shouldn't* raise our voices. Maybe we *shouldn't* reach across divides. Maybe we *shouldn't* advocate for change. Maybe we *shouldn't* love the people who are different from us. Maybe we *shouldn't*.

But I don't really care who the world says we *should* be. I'm done trying to live a life I *should* be living. Instead, I want to live the life I was born to live. I want to break all the rules. I want to defy all the odds. I want to challenge everything the world expects from us young leaders.

We can be the people who dare to defy all the old, rigid rules.

I believe it's time for our generation to rise up and refuse to settle for the safe, cozy lives society tells us to chase after. And if we choose to live a distinct life, a life that really matters, our world will take notice. Some people will judge us, and some people will laugh at us. But it will be because deep down, they desire to live a beautiful, daring life as well.

The invitation to live a life that matters comes from Jesus. It's a costly, deeply painful, and heart-wrenching call. And it's a freeing, wild, risky, adventurous call. It's both. But it's what our hearts were created to long for. The very same God who trusted Peter and Andrew to start the movement of the early church is the very same God beckoning to the young leaders of today, inviting us to start a movement in our world and in our culture here, right now.

This season of our lives as young leaders isn't just preparation for our lives. This *is* our lives.

GENERATION
DISTINCT

"WE CAN BE THE PEOPLE WHO DARE
TO DEFY ALL THE OLD, RIGID RULES."

If Jesus Christ trusted the launch and leadership of the most important movement of all time to a circle of ordinary teens and twentysomethings, then why couldn't He use the young leaders of today to lead our culture into a brand-new kind of future once again?

Because Jesus sees the world differently. He chooses the unlikely in our world. He sees past what the world sees to uncover the person He knows you could be. He is reaching out to you, drawing you out of your mediocrity and inviting you into meaning. He is calling you out of ordinary and giving you the gift of extraordinary. You are being shaken out of normal and drawn into a radical new way of life. This is your invitation to get out of your boat. This is your invitation to walk away from your normal. This is your invitation to leave everything behind and set out on a brand-new journey to discover a brand-new way to live.

You have the potential to live a life that matters.

MOVEMENT #2

CRAFT YOUR PASSION

Discover the Wrong You Were Born to Make Right

ON THE LAST DAY OF OUR TRIP to Colorado Springs, Faith and I decided to try just one more hike. We figured the past few days of hiking and climbing had prepared us for any kind of trail Colorado could throw at us. So, without much research or prep work, we laced up our shoes, grabbed our half-full water bottles and a Clif Bar, and ran out the door with anticipation.

We were in high spirits—and then we arrived at the base of the Incline. "The Incline," as it's dubbed, is considered an extreme trail, gaining nearly two thousand feet of elevation in less than one mile. The sight of it made us sweat and shift nervously and look back over our shoulders to see if it was too late to catch a ride back to the Springs. Our gaze slowly followed the trail higher, and higher, and higher, to the top of the mountain buried deep in the whipped white spring clouds. Then we looked back at each other. There we stood. Underprepared, under-qualified, and overly ambitious. The path stretched out in front of us, mocking us for our naivete.

At this point, the only thing we could do was take a step. So that is exactly what we did. We took our first step and, just like that, our adventure began.

We struggled up the mountain. Every thirty steps or so, we would collapse onto a nearby rock or tree branch, our Chicago lungs screaming at us for bringing them to such a high altitude. We would then give each other a motivating pep talk, worthy to be recorded in a sports movie pregame scene, and proceed to climb thirty more steps. Before we were halfway up the mountain, we felt beat. Our legs were burning. Faith, who has asthma, didn't have her inhaler. We had run out of water.

But we continued to climb. Breathe in. Breathe out. Breathe in. Breathe out. The way back was narrow and filled with people climbing up, making it impossible to turn around and go down. So we just continued to climb. As we approached the halfway point, we noticed a gathering of people. Their voices were thick with the sound of a decision. As we drew nearer, we discovered the source of their conflict.

There, taunting us with promises of comfort and ease, was what the locals call "the Bailout."

Halfway up this legendary climb, the Bailout is the easy out, a downward trail away from the remaining stairs. The Bailout can be a wise choice for people who realize partway through the climb that their health is in danger in one way or another. But it's also known for tripping up and defeating even the most committed of hikers. After all, why would you choose to push yourself, stretch yourself, wear yourself out when you can tap out halfway up and take the scenic route back down the mountain?

We were exhausted, but we decided to continue our climb, pushing aside the temptation of a way out for one important reason: We saw the goal in front of us. The top loomed before us, cheering us on, inviting us higher and higher with each step. The end point was visible and attainable. We knew where we were going.

Eventually, we looked up and realized we were almost to our goal. We were excited (and maybe just a little bit cocky). We had done it! We were just about to reach the summit, the peak, the victory! But then . . . as we reached what we had always thought was our goal, we looked up. Up. There was still more *up*. We didn't understand. We thought we knew our goal and our aim. But everything we thought we were reaching for, moving toward deliberately, step by step, was wrong.

A middle-aged man, weathered and sneering, passed us on the trail and laughed. "You got fooled. This here is the false summit."

The false summit. The *false* summit. From the ground, this spot appears to be the top. The goal. But it isn't. Once you reach the false summit, you face hundreds of the steepest steps on the trail before you reach the actual top of the mountain. We felt empty, discouraged knots form in our stomachs.

Have you ever arrived at a point on your journey when you looked around and realized that everything you were doing to try to make a difference didn't seem to be changing anything? The world was still dark. Injustice was just as pervasive as ever. And your little life wasn't making any sort of a dent. Maybe you wanted to create intentional relationships with your neighbors, and you thought you were making progress, but now they close their apartment door when they see you coming. Maybe you spent weeks investing in the single mom living on the street in your city, but all of a sudden one day she was gone, and you felt discouraged. Maybe you emailed a local nonprofit to volunteer to welcome refugees into your community . . . and they never emailed you back. Maybe you started mentoring a freshman on your campus who is drowning in depression, but he or she has become distant and doesn't seem to even appreciate your investment. You want to change the world, but when it's not quite as simple as you thought it would be, it's easy to take the bailout path.

When things get hard, we want to quit. We give up. We wonder if justice, impact, purpose, fulfillment, and passion are just words plastered on billboards and promised in commercials and promoted on the front of three-dollar journals. We don't know what else to do. So we settle into a routine that is safer, that doesn't require so much sacrifice, that won't demand such deep levels of surrender.

But if we ever want to discover a different way to live, then it's time to make some changes.

So let's reject the bailout path,
refuse the defeat of the false summit,
push though the hard,
create some strategy,
aim higher.

It's time to discover the wrong we were born to make right.

Faith and I sat down on the false summit, gasping for breath and wiping beads of sweat off our foreheads, warm from the bright Colorado spring sunshine. We kicked the dirt and shoved our empty water bottles into our backpacks.

We had a choice to make. Were we willing to reimagine our goal and continue this journey? Were we willing to accept and own the fact that our goal was harder to reach than we thought it would be?

Would we let our feelings of defeat and disappointment derail us, or would we stand up, re-create our goal, and start again?

We high-fived. We stood up. We looked up. Now we knew where we were going. No more "false summits." No more lies. We were clear, and we had a renewed sense of purpose. We would reach the top, no matter what. One foot after the other. One step, then another. It seemed so simple. Yet it was the only way to arrive at our destination. One step, then another.

With our goal in mind, we were soon a mere fifty steps away from the real summit. Suddenly, the passion, the adrenaline, and the excitement filled us with a renewed sense of urgency. We shouted to each other, "No stopping now! We are making it to the top. No more breaks. Let's do it now!"

We ran up the final steps. I can remember the moment in slow motion. Taking the final step and breathing out as I finally saw the top of the mountain. Turning around, my breath catching in my throat at the beauty and magnitude of the view. The satisfaction of knowing we'd reached our goal. And, most of all, the experience that was already becoming a sweet, treasured memory of an adventure never to be forgotten.

As we stood there, immersed in the magic of the Colorado Rockies, we did not wish we had chosen to do something easier that day. We did not wish we had stayed safe and cozy on the ground. We did not wish we had taken the bailout trail halfway up the mountain. We were glad, and so grateful, that we had chosen the adventurous path laid out in front of us that day.

There is a path in front of you. A calling. A purpose. A wrong you were born to make right. You. Not your friend, or your parent, or your spouse, or your pastor, or your boss. *You.* You will never regret choosing the path you were born to live. Never. It will be hard. You may be tempted to abandon the path. You may find your goals aren't quite right and you have to start all over again. But don't take the bailout. Re-create your vision. Keep fighting. Keep showing up. As you persevere, you discover a life you never dreamed was possible.

Are you ready to discover it?

THE RING

I think God has a special place in His heart for people who are on the run, fleeing crises in their countries. My friend Jessica had to escape Burma as a refugee when she was fifteen years old. I picture her sitting down with Jesus one day and hearing Him say, "Me too. I remember what it felt like to run and flee.[1] You are seen and known."

The struggle and pain of displaced people is one of

the greatest humanitarian crises raging in our world. I knew I couldn't just sit back and watch it happen. I had to do *something*. At first, I thought this meant I had to travel halfway around the world to visit a refugee camp. But it turns out I was wrong. Fighting injustice doesn't have to include a plane ride. More often than not, it just looks like hanging out with kids in your own backyard.

I found an organization working with refugees right in my own community. They empowered me and prepared me to do what I could right where I was. They connected me with an elementary school in an area where a lot of refugee families live. Once a week, I'd hang out with these refugee kids for an hour to help them with homework, hear their stories, love them well, build relationships, and communicate, "You're wanted here."

At first, I didn't know what to expect. I walked in very unprepared and somewhat naive. And that is when I met Chen. Chen was a third grader with a mischievous smile and big, curious brown eyes. She giggled easily. And from the very first day I walked into that school, she made me feel welcome. *She* made *me* feel welcome. She taught me that welcome is not just something you extend to people who look like you, or talk like you, or come from the same background as you. It's for everyone.

One day, she bounded over to me with extra

amounts of gusto and exclaimed, "Hannah! Hannah! I have something for you!"

I laughed. "Show me, Chen!" I expected to see the kind of beautiful art that could only come from a spunky third grader, complete with bright colors and exuberant doodles. But instead, she reached out a closed fist. Slowly, she opened her palm—and there in her sweet, small hand was a plastic ring.

"Chen, what do you mean? Is this for *me*?" Why in the world would *she* give a gift to *me*?

"I wanted to get this for you. My mom brought me to the store, and I used my own money to buy this for you. It's yours."

Tears welled up in my eyes. In a world where justice seems complicated and hard and political, Chen understood what justice really means. In a world where she was called unwelcome and out of place, Chen was demonstrating sacrificial love.

I remember friends questioning my decision to volunteer with these refugee children. They told me, "You are so busy leading Generation Distinct. Are you sure you want to add this to your schedule?"

In reality, I recognize this time with the students required very little sacrifice from me. The amount of sacrifice doesn't matter—rather, the very act of sacrifice communicates where your heart really lies.

Chen taught me something I will never forget: Real love requires surrender. Sacrifice is the source of all sustainable justice. Unity only arrives when we abdicate our advantage.

Fighting injustice seems appealing until we actually do it. The stories plastered on our Facebook walls, posted on our Twitter feeds, and highlighted on the news channels hardly ever highlight the messy parts of fighting injustice.

Thousands of people watched Mother Teresa win the Nobel Peace Prize. But they didn't watch her walk through the impoverished streets of Calcutta, wearing shoes too small for her feet, trying to love people who often refused to receive her help.

We have been inspired by Dr. Martin Luther King Jr.'s famous "I Have a Dream" speech. But far fewer of us have studied the letters he wrote from a bleak prison cell after he was arrested for speaking out against racial inequality.

We love the story of an old, weathered William Wilberforce finally witnessing the abolition of slavery in the British Empire. We rarely talk, however, about all it cost him during the painful forty-six years it took to see this injustice defeated.

If we want to join the fight for justice because it seems glamorous, we're in for a rude awakening. Bringing justice into places of injustice never ensures a life of ease, or glamour, or comfort. The only promise it makes is that our lives will never be the same. We will experience deep pain, be called

"UNITY ONLY ARRIVES WHEN WE
ABDICATE OUR ADVANTAGE."

on to make great sacrifices, and be confronted with real risk. We will be asked to give more than we expected, and we will rarely see success. We will meet real people who live amid shocking suffering. And we will carry heavier burdens than we previously thought possible.

But if we say yes . . .

if we join the fight . . .

if we show up . . .

if we surrender everything . . .

if we sacrifice all we are . . .

if we risk our comfort . . .

if we enter the mess . . .

if we welcome the burden . . .

we will experience a deeper fulfillment than we ever dreamed possible.

Because we weren't designed to experience fulfillment the way society says we should. Rather, you and I were created with a wrong we were born to make right. And if our Creator so lovingly gifted us with such important purpose, it is no wonder we only find our deepest fulfillment and greatest joy when living within that purpose.

LISTENING TO THE WRONG VOICES

My phone alarm vibrates next to my head, and I reach to grab it before I open my eyes, knocking the water glass off the nightstand and jamming my finger on the heavy base of the lamp. My eyes pop open at the pain, and I roll onto my back, trying to muster the self-will to jump up. Instead, I pull up my phone and open Twitter. I know I shouldn't. According to the latest BuzzFeed article, it's the worst way to start your morning. Oh well. I'll start heeding that advice tomorrow.

I start scrolling and liking the tweets that make me laugh and retweeting the quotes I think are clever. And then I see a new hashtag that started trending while I was sleeping. #PrayFor . . . My heart starts racing, and I sit up. I click on the hashtag and find the article about what happened. The pictures are horrifying. I'm awake now, though I wish I could just go back to sleep and forget. But I can't. Because I've been slapped in the face by the injustice and the pain and the evil permeating our world. It feels distant, yet it feels so personal. It feels out of my control, yet it feels all too real.

I put my phone down. I slowly get up. I don't really know what to do next. It would be easier to be naive. It would be simpler to be uninformed. My soul feels like a hard rock of burden and confusion in the center of my chest. I slip on a sweater and grab my old, worn Bible.

I make some coffee because that feels normal. And when the world is scary, I feel the need for some normal.

I wander outside in the first whispers of sunrise. I hold my steaming-hot cup of coffee with both hands and allow the silence of morning to wash over me. I need space to process. I need time to grieve. I need to sit in the discomfort and allow my soul to mourn the injustice, the hate, and the disunity of our world.

Slowly, I open my leather-backed Bible. Honestly, I have little hope I will find anything that can meet me where I am today.

I don't think it's wrong if we doubt God. I do think it's wrong if we allow that doubt to prevent us from exploring the depths of God.

Without any direction or plan, I find myself entrenched in the story of the prophet Jeremiah. And there, sitting before me, in the very Bible I've opened a thousand times, is a chapter I have never noticed before. One that puts words to the stirrings of my soul.

"This is what the LORD says: Do what is just and right. Rescue from the hand of the oppressor the one who has been robbed. Do no wrong or violence to the foreigner, the fatherless or the widow, and do not shed innocent blood in this place. . . ."

"Woe to him who builds his palace by unrighteousness,
    his upper rooms by injustice,
making his own people work for nothing,

not paying them for their labor.
He says, 'I will build myself a great palace
with spacious upper rooms.'
So he makes large windows in it,
panels it with cedar
and decorates it in red.

"Does it make you a king
to have more and more cedar?
Did not your father have food and drink?
He did what was right and just,
so all went well with him.
He defended the cause of the poor and needy,
and so all went well.
Is this not what it means to know me?"
declares the LORD.

JEREMIAH 22:3, 13-16

We try so hard to build our great "palaces." We work and we strive and we build and we run toward the perfect and beautiful life. We compare our lives to the world's standard of the "good life" and complain that ours is less than perfect. We feel entitled.

But who told us that? Who told us that is how life is meant to be lived? What if we *are* told how life is truly meant to be lived . . . but we're ignoring it? What if we've already been shown the goals and purposes of our lives, but we're so busy pursuing the things we think we deserve that we're completely missing them? What if Jesus is giving us the blueprints of a life that matters, but we're so busy building a life according to the world that we're missing it all together?

> "This is what the LORD says: Do what is just and right. Rescue from the hand of the oppressor the one who has been robbed. Do no wrong or violence to the foreigner, the fatherless or the widow."

Maybe we're asking the wrong questions entirely.

Maybe, if we were sitting down face-to-face with Jesus, our conversation would look strikingly different. Maybe He would ask, "Are you fighting for what is just? Are you working for what is right? Are you rescuing real people out of oppression? Are you providing for individuals who are struggling to make ends meet? Are you standing up for the rights of the foreigner? Are you caring for the orphans in your town or around the world? Are you showing up for the widow in your family who is lonely? Are you defending the cause of people who have no opportunity to defend themselves? Are you an agent of my love in this world? Are you telling the people around you about everything you have found in me?"

I'm learning something I never knew before. Maybe our perfect houses, perfect lives, perfect image, perfect posts, perfect schedules, perfect routines, perfect meals will not change the world. Because they will not be here forever. They will not matter in eternity.

Do you know what will matter? PEOPLE. The sacrifices we made for PEOPLE. The love we showed to PEOPLE. The resources we gave up for PEOPLE. The time we poured into PEOPLE.

If the news is ever going to look different, it has to start with us. When we fight for justice, we change the narrative of our world. When we stand up for the oppressed, we change the narrative of our world. When we speak out for the forgotten, we change the narrative of our world. When we honor the image of God in every human being, we change the narrative of our world. When we show unprecedented kinds of love, we change the narrative of our world.

I don't want to drown in the hashtags and the news and the hate and the evil and the headlines and the messages trying to tell me our world is too far gone.

William Wilberforce once said, "We can no longer plead ignorance, we cannot evade it; it is now an object placed before us; we cannot pass it; we may spurn it, we may kick it out of our way, but we cannot turn aside so as to avoid seeing it."[2]

Friends, we see the injustice. And it's breaking our hearts. It's bringing deep mourning. It's threatening our hope. And it feels like it's tearing our world apart. But I refuse to believe that is the end of the story.

Instead, I believe this is the very moment when we step up anyway. This is the very moment when we need to cling to hope even tighter. This is the moment when we decide a more beautiful world is still possible, and we are going to be part of fighting for it.

So let's engage in what is happening in our world. Let's become informed about it, mourn it, talk about it, raise our voices about it. Because it's not enough to throw up our hands and sigh and say, "The world is just a mess." It's not enough to turn off the news and say, "Someone else can do something."

As we choose to live out of a deep love for the people in this world who are hurting, oppressed, forgotten, betrayed, abandoned, and abused, we start to roll up our sleeves, walk into our culture, and actually do something about the injustice and the pain and the sorrow and the fear. We choose to make wrong things right.

We come up with real solutions. We fight for systemic change. We look to empower people instead of making them dependent on our heroic generosity. We see them as people instead of projects. We show up again and again and again and create relationships with people who are suffering. We ask questions instead of thinking we know the solutions. We create sustainable change and fix broken systems. We look people in the eye and ask them how we can help. We see past the pain and the injustice and the oppression and the brokenness, and we see the humanity within every person. We build bridges across divides and divisions the world has created. And we treat every individual with dignity and honor. Every. Single. Time.

Because that's just what love is all about. It shows up when it doesn't make sense, when everything seems too far gone, when the injustice feels too dark, and it brings light and hope and beauty back to our world.

JUST START

I wasn't fooling any of the seasoned climbers when I walked into the gym on a frosty January day with my shiny, spotless, brand-new gear. I was a climbing virgin. And everybody knew it.

I nervously pulled out my harness, wondering if I should have any idea what to do with all the straps and loops. I put on my shoes, and then I took them off. They hurt. It felt like squeezing back into your favorite jeans after holiday weekends spent in sweatpants. Wrong. Too tight, too small, too wrong.

I put the shoes back on, wobbling over to the first wall like a newborn foal discovering her legs. I looked around, hoping to somehow convince everyone that

I belonged. What really gave me away, however, was the fact that I had no idea what to do.

I had all the right gear. I was at the right place. I was even putting my hands on the holds. But I wasn't climbing. I was still just standing on the ground, dreaming about what it would feel like to climb, to be a rock climber, to reach the top of the wall.

I think we all want to be people who are living out our passions. We want to be advocates of justice. We want to be known as people who care. We want to experience what it would feel like to make real impact in the world. But, as we reflect on the life we're living, it quickly becomes apparent we aren't doing anything of lasting impact.

We're in the right place. We have all the gear we need. We are reading the books and doing the research. We watched the videos on Facebook, and we liked the tweets on Twitter. We have a shirt that says *Justice* in an artsy font. Our coffee mug has a map of the world on it. We bought fair-trade tea last week.

But, if we were honest, we'd acknowledge that we're really just standing on the ground with no idea what to do or where to start.

It's okay to be there. But it's not okay to *stay* there. If you want to go on a journey to craft that passion, to take ownership of your life, to say yes to create impact in the world, there are three steps you can take to craft your passion.

STEP 1: DO SOMETHING

It was the day of Generation Distinct's very first board meeting. I was borrowing the conference room of another organization, preparing for my incredible, brilliant board members to walk in for a discussion about vision, budgets, business plans, policies, legal procedures, and more. I had stayed up until 3:00 a.m. nearly every night that week preparing. I was exhausted. But I was ready, and the adrenaline from what this meeting meant for the future of Generation Distinct had set in.

My staff began to arrive. I love my staff. They're wild dreamers and crazy risk takers. And they're some of my deepest friends. I'm also a fierce people person—so in the midst of prepping for this important meeting, I ran out the front door to greet my staff with hugs and excitement.

We walked inside the building and through the lobby, laughing and celebrating this milestone day for our new nonprofit. But when I reached to open the next door, the one that would let us into the space we were using, it didn't budge. It had locked behind me. And the keys were right there on the other side of the door.

My stomach dropped miles below the ground I was standing on. My palms began to sweat. I laughed nervously. I was locked out of my first board meeting. Our new board members—all impressive, sharp professionals—were arriving in thirty minutes. I was *nailing* the leadership thing.

Usually, my craziest ideas come in the moments of greatest urgency. I had thirty minutes to get inside that room. It was go time.

We started with rookie-level plans: trying other doors, calling the people who owned the building, wiggling bobby pins in the lock. Nothing worked. Then we looked up and noticed the ceiling wasn't plaster wall. It was made of ceiling tiles. Ceiling tiles could be moved. Ceiling tiles could be taken out.

We awkwardly dragged a table, the only piece of furniture in the vestibule, over to the inside door. The tallest of my staff members climbed on top of the table, reached as high as he could, and gingerly removed two small ceiling tiles from their metal framing. The stage was set.

My selfless friend clasped his hands together and hoisted me up into the ceiling. I rose past the remaining ceiling tiles and grabbed the pipes above me, dust and tile pieces raining down past me like a soft, musty December snow.

I laughed out loud, a mixture of nervous energy and true delight at the adventure this had become. There I sat, shoved up into the ceiling of this office building, only minutes before my board members were scheduled to arrive.

I focused on my mission and monkey-barred my way through the ceiling, swinging myself over the top of the door. White-knuckled, I clung to the brass pipes in the ceiling, hoping they would somehow bear my weight. Then, once I was somewhat confident of my hold, I removed the ceiling tiles on the other side of the doorframe and began to lower myself through. Using my feet to walk down the wall, I extended my arms, released my hold on the pipes and, finally, dropped to the ground.

It had worked. I was in. I started jumping up and down in victory, yelling out, "We're in! We're in!" and then unlocked the door for my staff. The relief set in, and I sighed deeply. Minutes later, our new board members arrived, and our meeting went on as planned. Everything went back into place and the building was no worse for the wear.

But I have never looked at ceiling tiles quite the same again.

We had an urgent, clear *why*. We had to get inside. We didn't know how to do it or where to start. But we didn't just wait until the perfect idea magically appeared. We started to do *something*. We tried and tried and tried again. And eventually, we just climbed through the ceiling.

I think it's time young people started climbing through the ceiling. Often, we become so consumed with *discovering* our passion that we never actually *do* anything about the injustice invading our world.

You want to know the injustice you are called to

combat. You deeply yearn to understand how God has uniquely equipped you to change the world. You are ready and hungry to discover how you can make an impact in the world. So . . . you wait. You wait for a prompting, or a whisper, or a sign, or a message to appear. You wait for a magical moment, when the ambient musical tones begin to play, and the fog appears, and a deep voice proclaims how you were born to change the world.

Or maybe we're just waiting because it's easier to use our lack of clarity as an excuse rather than actually doing something.

We're not taking action. We're standing in the lobby of our life. We aren't inside. We aren't outside. We are in the lobby. But life isn't meant to be lived in the lobby. We may have to climb through the ceiling to get where we need to go.

There is a wrong you were born to make right. And what if God has already given you everything you need to right that wrong in the world, live out your passions, fight for justice, and create lasting change? What if He is on the edge of His seat, watching to see what you are going to do with everything He's given you . . . but you're sitting back, waiting for a magical sign no one promised you? There is a wrong you were born to make right. And if that's the case, you owe it to our world to do something about it.

I meet with young people every week who ask me

"THERE IS A WRONG YOU
WERE BORN TO MAKE RIGHT."

the same question, "How do I discover my passion?" They look at me expectantly because I run an organization that empowers young leaders to discover their passions. They expect me to give them a fancy diagram or a detailed action plan. But I don't. Not at first. Because that's not what they need. They need to just. *do.* something.

Processes, strategies, and structures are important. We'll need them eventually. But that's not where we start.

Instead, we get off our couches, off our phones, out of our own little worlds, and we do something. Because, chances are, God is not going to reveal your passion to you as you sit on your couch, staring at the TV screen. You probably won't find it as you're mindlessly scrolling through social media. You won't discover the wrong you're born to make right as you sit in a bar complaining about your lack of clarity.

It is far more likely God will reveal your passion to you when your hands are dirty, your hair is messy, your body is tired, and your eyes are sparkling. When you're in the center of the fight, when you're in the midst of real injustice, when you're in the mess of real relationships—God will tap you on the shoulder and say, "That was it! What you just saw, what you just heard, what you just experienced, *that* was the wrong you were born to make right." It will be in the midst of the doing that you discover your passion.

It's time for us to climb through the ceiling. It's time to do *something*.

Get involved in stopping the human trafficking crisis. Run a 5K to raise money to build wells in communities with no access to clean water. Spend time talking to and learning from the beautiful people at a nursing home. Mentor an at-risk student. Make a meal for a family living below the poverty line in your town. Show up at the same street corner every weekend to form a relationship with a homeless family. Volunteer to invest in individuals with special needs. Get involved with an organization that helps refugee families adapt to an overwhelmingly new culture. Encourage the middle schooler on your block who is about to give up hope. Sell your stuff and give the money to sponsor a child in a developing country. Open your home to a high schooler who lives in a toxic environment. Start a company to provide jobs for the homeless. Visit people in prison. Partner with an organization to advocate for the rights of slaves around the world. Talk to your government about laws that need to change. Learn from someone who is different from you. Become a foster parent to care for children caught in a broken system. Raise money to build a school for girls in another country who have no access to education.

I don't know what you've been created to do, but I do know there is so much exciting and beautiful work to be done. God is inviting us to be a part of what He is doing in the world. So don't miss your unique place in it. Because there's just too much at stake.

There is a wrong you were born to make right. There is a passion God has placed inside of you. You have everything you need to take action, to move toward it, to try all the things and figure it out. Even if you have to climb through the ceiling.

The first step is to do something.

The second step is to keep doing something.

STEP 2: KEEP DOING SOMETHING

When I was nine, my favorite summer pastime was catching frogs. My friends would come over and we would venture into the pond behind my house, usually losing yet another pair of flip-flops in the suction-like mud at the edge of the grimy water. But the mud and the missing flip-flops didn't bother us as long as we caught frogs.

We would place the amphibians in large plastic bins and gather anything we thought might bring some comfort to our slimy friends. Grass, rocks, leftover lunch, dead bugs—it all went into the bins. We would spend hours with those frogs. We trained them. We held them. We set them free in the grass, and then ran after them again as we squealed and giggled. We loved catching frogs—and we had big plans for them.

We made a flyer that read, *We will capture all of the frogs in your window wells. Cost: $10. (We get to keep all the frogs.)*

Our plan, we thought, was near genius. We would pass out these flyers around the neighborhood and make money so we could purchase finer equipment for our new endeavor—bigger nets and better plastic bins. Plus, we'd have more frogs.

We were determined. This was our new passion.

Until it wasn't. We moved on to another interest, another exciting venture, another day.

At nine years old, I discovered something I still need to be reminded of today. Sustaining our passion is more difficult than making the decision to pursue a new passion. We love *starting* things. We love the excitement and thrill of the *beginning*. We love the fresh *start* and idealistic *possibilities*. We love the adrenaline rush that comes with *new*.

You know what isn't glamorous? Sustained passion. Commitment. Consistency. Showing up day, after day, after day. But do you know what actually ushers justice into our world? Sustained passion. Commitment. Consistency. Showing up day, after day, after day.

We love the notion that we could pick up and move at the drop of a hat. We idolize a lifestyle that allows us to travel from place to place. We dream of a nomad existence, wandering to and fro, without any commitments. But we often forget one of the central principles of creating impact in our world.

Impact is all about people. And if we want to have an impact on the lives of real people, we have to actually be present in their lives. We need to show up consistently. We need to be with them in the pain. We need to invite them into our lives. We need to do life alongside them.

When Jesus invited Peter to leave his boat, He could have said, "Come, obey Me." Or, "Come, read My laws." Or, "Come with Me, and I'll grab a meal with you, just this once." But He didn't. He said, "Come, follow Me." He was inviting Peter to join His life. To be a part of His story. To live in a sustained, long-term, committed relationship.

Jesus knows that life change rarely happens through one free meal, one brief interaction, or one surface-level conversation. It happens through consistency. It happens though life-on-life investment. It happens when we show up, time after time after time, in the lives of the people we are called to love and lead to Jesus.

If we start investing in the homeless family who lives down the road from us, we don't just hand them a meal and leave. We show up every weekend. We learn their names. We hear their stories. We ask them questions. We look them in the eyes. We tell them they matter.

If we start to create a relationship with the refugees

72

in our community, we don't just donate a couch for their apartment. We knock on their door. We introduce ourselves. We welcome them into our community. We ask if they want to grab a meal together. We ask about their lives. We keep showing up.

If we start to invest in high school students, or serve at a nursing home, or create relationships with girls walking the street, or start an after-school club for at-risk youth, we *must* keep showing up, again and again and again and again. We ask them what they need and don't assume we know it all. We love them through our consistency—which means we'll have to plant our roots.

Create relationships, invest in lives, show up consistently, and you will usher real justice into our world. Watching Jesus transform lives, communities, cities, and nations through your faithfulness and consistency and intentional love may prove to be the greatest adventure you ever embark on.

The first step is to do something.

The second step is to keep doing something.

The third step is to listen loudly and listen softly.

STEP 3: LISTEN LOUDLY AND LISTEN SOFTLY

When Generation Distinct began, we didn't have the budget to invest in an office building. So, naturally, I found myself spending much of my life in coffee shops.

Most of my workdays began to the tune of soft, folksy music laced with the purr of an espresso machine and underscored by the gentle murmur of voices.

Each seat in a coffee shop tells a story. Young college students flip the pages of their textbooks, scribbling frantic notes in the margins and nervously tapping pens against sweaty temples. Entrepreneurs type furiously, making last-minute changes to their business plan for the investor who is about to walk through the door. Bloggers are writing articles, and artists are marketing their work. Songwriters are uploading their music, and CEOs are strategizing for their next meeting. Photographers in a competitive market are sitting side by side, sharing ideas and tips with crisp white mugs in hand. Old friends meet up after years apart, and new friends connect for the first time to share their stories and dreams and plans for the future.

And honestly . . . it all feels a little like church to me. It's a sacred space where creativity is being unleashed, ideas are becoming realities, and dreams are being hatched. It's at little café tables in coffee shops in my own hometown where I first began to tell my friends about the crazy dreams bouncing around in my mind. These friends made space for me to process and create and dream without fear of being judged. Quickly, they would begin to enter the dream themselves, and we'd spend hours dreaming up wild ideas of what it would mean to empower young people to live lives that matter (and we'd often get kicked out of the shop at closing time). They would furiously take notes and challenge me to dream bigger and bring fresh ideas and build new realities. We'd create so fast, we were speaking over ourselves.

This small tribe of friends, sitting across from me amid the hum of a coffee-shop crowd, would listen intently and nod their heads and simply say, "I'm in."

That's a true friend—a friend who can say "I'm in" before they really know what they're in for. Because they're not just in when it's easy and established and exciting and impressive. They're in when it's messy and new and unknown and scary. They're not just in for the product. They're in for the process.

I think sometimes God speaks in the silence. But other times, especially for a loud people person like me, I think He speaks in the midst of relationships. We don't get to dictate when or how God speaks. He just speaks.

This is how I best listen to God. It's through talking and sharing and processing and discussing and hearing truth from the mouths of my people. God speaks when I make space to listen loudly.

So talk to your tribe. Ask them questions. Process your experiences. Share the stirrings in your soul. Invite them into your dreams. Test your ideas by their wisdom. Listen to the truth they speak. Test them by the truth of Jesus. Receive their challenges. Speak your fears. Express your doubts. Celebrate your discoveries. Listen loudly.

And then listen softly. Compare your newly realized passion to what God has already said in the Bible. Pray for a heart of surrender. Invite the Holy Spirit to refine your passion. And continue these disciplines every single day.

The first step is to do something.

The second step is to keep doing something.

The third step is to listen loudly and listen softly.

Don't wait. Start now. Take the first step. Because there is simply too much that hangs in the balance.

What hangs in the balance?

- the innocence of young girls who are victims of sex trafficking;
- the safety of children thrown into a broken foster care system;
- the lives of orphans neglected and alone;
- the dignity of people who are told they are *less* because of the color of their skin;
- the safety of families fleeing danger in their countries, searching for a place to call home;
- the lives of teenagers struggling with depression and sometimes even attempting suicide;
- the redemption of families caught in a cycle of addiction;
- the future of girls who will likely not have access to education because of their gender;

- the health of a baby born in a country with no access to clean water; and
- the eternities of real people.

This isn't an *if you want, if you have time, extracurricular activity* kind of thing. This is a *sacrifice all of yourself, risk everything you have, give from the deepest parts of your soul, fight with an unwavering tenacity, leave no part of yourself in the safety of comfort* kind of thing.

Refuse to back down, to quit, or to retreat. Stay on the front lines of this fight. There is a wrong you were born to make right. So go out and start. And keep going. And listen. And, if you have to, don't be afraid to climb through the ceiling.

RIDING THE WAVES

I truly thought I was born to be a surfer. I'm not even joking. I was utterly convinced I would one day wake up and become an incredible surfer, to the point that I had surfing decor on my dresser and T-shirts that told the world I was a surfer. If I saw a surfer on the beach while I was traveling, I would literally walk up to them and talk as though I were one of them.

The only problem was . . . I had never actually gone surfing.

So when I finally had the opportunity to try my hand at the sport, I grabbed a board, took a deep breath, and walked into the water. Surfing was nothing like I expected and everything I had hoped for, the most terrifying experience and the most amazing thrill, all at the same time. It was both the most stretching activity I had ever tried and the most natural expression of who I was all in one paradoxical experience.

I can still feel the salty water, fierce and strong and turbulent. I can still feel the cold rush on my skin as I plunged beneath the depths of the icy blue waves, only to pop up again, gasping for breath. I remember the frustration of the missed waves and the laughter after many awkward attempts. I remember being exhausted.

But the most vivid, brightly colored memory I have of that day is the first magical moment when everything clicked. The moment when I stood up on my board and, suddenly, I was riding on top of the water. The mist splashed my face, and my smile grew. In an instant, I found joy and whimsy and beauty in the midst of the turbulence.

And I think that's what Jesus longs to do in your life and in mine. He never promised that living out our passion would be easy or safe or comfortable. He never promised if we created real impact in the world, He would take away all of the turbulence. Instead, I think He longs to give us a place to stand, to soar, to thrive amid the wild waves of our world. I think He longs to lift us above the icy water and pour joy deep into our souls. I think the suffering and the beauty can all be rolled into one significant life. It's what He showed us from the beginning.

As He hung on the cross, beaten, bruised, spit on, humiliated, tortured, Jesus was a paradox of suffering and beauty. He was living the life He was born to live. He was accomplishing the task He was created to complete. He was living out the very will of His Father. And yet—He was in the middle of profound suffering.

I can't promise that following Jesus will lead you into an enjoyable life. I can't promise that following the most revolutionary, radical leader of all time will lead you into a safe and cozy routine that *feels* good. I don't want to pretend this life of giving everything we are and everything we have over to the God of the universe ensures success or thrill or esteem or fun.

If we follow the One whose beautiful life of purpose led Him to a cross, we must be prepared for deep sacrifice and real cost. Because that's exactly what His life looked like. Paradox. Beauty and pain. Joy and sacrifice. Purpose and cost. Life to the full, and life given away.

So grab your board and get in the water. You may get knocked down, or tossed about, or struck with the waves. But don't be discouraged. This world needs you. And God wants to equip you with everything you need to make wrongs right, in every paradoxical part of it.

And when you find that perfect wave, ride it. Stand strong and embrace the whimsy and the magic and the beauty of crafting your passion, fighting for justice, and unleashing lasting impact in our world.

MOVEMENT #3

FIND YOUR PEOPLE

Link Arms in Unity

ON A RECENT TRIP FOR A CONFERENCE, I found myself walking through the airport, following the signs above my head in a maze past hundreds and hundreds of all different kinds of people. Businesswomen in high heels wheeled their shiny black suitcases, frazzled parents hustled after their toddlers as brightly colored bags hung off every available limb, and young adventurers spoke into their iPhone cameras as they chronicled their latest trip for their online fans. Eventually, I found my way to the baggage claim and waited for the motor to groan the announcement that our bags were on their way. I'm known for being many things in my friend group: loud, enthusiastic, passionate, and determined to dress in a way that makes people say, "Can you really wear that?" Push the boundaries? Sure. Shake up the normal? Absolutely. So needless to say, understated is not one of my signatures. Which actually comes in handy when searching for your luggage on the conveyor belt. Black suitcase after black suitcase passed by me, and then a flash of color emerged, and I knew my luggage had arrived. I walked up and slid the neon suitcase off the conveyor belt and turned to walk away.

But then I noticed a sweet older couple running toward the baggage claim in a frantic hustle. They didn't speak much of my language, but I could tell from their worried tones that they had missed their luggage. They paused to scan the conveyor belt for their suitcase, then spotted it and started to hustle again, chasing a suitcase around the oval-shaped baggage claim at a hilariously hopeless speed.

I placed my suitcase to the side and ran over to help. I caught up to them just as they had gotten their hands on their bag. They pulled and pulled, but the power of the motor overpowered their small frames. Eventually I stepped in, smiled, gently reached over to yank the suitcase off the luggage merry-go-round, and placed it safely beside the couple, who now looked as though they had just completed their first marathon.

"Here you go!" I smiled at them and began to walk away.

"Wow!" I heard one of them say.

I looked back and realized they were staring at me.

"It was really no problem," I said, amused that my mediocre strength had so impressed them. "Have a great trip." Again, I turned to walk away.

They called out, "Thank you! Thank you!" As I glanced back again, they waved, and the woman, strangely in awe of my ordinary strength, called out after me, "You must be Wonder Woman!"

I'm going to be honest—I loved that they called me Wonder Woman. I walked out of that airport as though I *were* the superhero who had broken into the boys' club and defended the townspeople while my gold headband flashed and my red cape flapped in the wind.

I think there is something deep within us all that wants to believe we can be the hero of our own story. It's why little girls and boys tie sheets around their necks and run around the room with their fists in the air. It's why we show up to the movie theater every time the new superhero movie comes out. It's why, every Halloween, grown men and women dress up in tights and masks and armor.

Deep within ourselves, we believe we are the heroes of our own story and that at some point, everyone else will wake up and discover just how incredible we really are. We don't expect it to be when we pull luggage off a conveyor belt, but I don't think we really care how it happens. We just believe we are *meant* to be the hero. At least, I do.

After all. I *am* Wonder Woman.

THOSE PEOPLE

If we were to gather a group of young adults in a room and ask them, "How do you fight for justice?" chances are we would hear a smattering of responses.

"Buy fair-trade coffee."

"Hand a sandwich out to the homeless."

"Talk about it on social media."

"Wear a T-shirt that supports a good cause."

"Pass out Thanksgiving meals every November."

"Volunteer at a homeless shelter every few months."

And those are not bad answers. They just don't capture the magnitude of what is really required to usher justice into our world. We love justice. We love being people who care about justice. We love being considered advocates for justice. Just as long as it doesn't actually change anything about the way we live.

Just as long as justice remains an activity we add into our lives when it feels convenient,

and doesn't interfere with the rest of our rhythms and routines,

and is still an extra-credit activity for those really good people, and doesn't interfere with our self-care,

and doesn't affect our bank accounts,

and is something we can engage in when it feels good for us,

. . . then we love justice.

If we are the heroes of our own stories, we get to engage in justice when it makes us look good. We can all of a sudden care about justice when we feel the need or when it's cool to post about it on social media. We can show up to the shelter, or the event, or the food pantry, or the street corner when it fits into our schedule, when it fits into our lives, or when it gives us the thrill that we're doing something that matters.

We *get* to be the hero. And, let's be honest, it feels really good to be the hero.

A few years ago, while I was traveling, I found myself sitting in the auditorium of a church with a fairly young congregation. It was a cool church, and it was clear they were growing at a rapid pace. The lobby buzzed with energy as young people sipped their coffee and caught up with friends. When I walked in, they welcomed me and showed me around and introduced me to some bright-eyed twentysomethings who talked about how much they loved their community at this church. They gave me a mug and one more handshake, and I wandered into the auditorium.

I found a seat in the middle and sat down on the edge of the row. I looked around at the empty auditorium because, let's be honest, people who are new to the church are always the first to sit down.

Eventually, the music began to play. As the auditorium filled with people, I tried to sing along to the unfamiliar songs they were playing. When we sat, a young man in a collared shirt and camel-colored suede boots jumped up on stage with gusto to give the announcements for the day.

He talked about the small-group sign-ups and the young-adult gathering taking place after the service and the baptisms coming up in two weeks. But when he shifted gears, I looked up from my coffee and listened closely.

"Did you know," he began, "that there are families here in our very own community who struggle to make ends meet?" He paused dramatically. "Did you know there are children who won't have new shoes for their first day of school? Did you know there are parents who can't provide meals for their children? Did you know there are people who actually live below the poverty line right here in our own backyard?"

He looked around the room, and so did I. That's when I saw it. The auditorium was full of twenty- and thirtysomethings shaking their heads in disbelief.

"It's shocking," the man continued. "But it doesn't have to be this way." He went on to share the extremely honorable aspiration their church had to raise money for at-need families in their community. This vision was good and right in so many ways. The heart behind this church truly was to help and serve and love the people in their community. But I sensed a mentality we can all easily fall into, one that threatens to strip any unity from our conversations around justice. The hero mentality.

The hero mentality is the belief that *we* were created to be God's helpers in the world, while others were created to be the helped. We get to wear the capes for the distressed townspeople who wait for us to rescue them. And, if we're transparent, we'd admit that we really like being the ones wearing the capes.

Without even realizing it, the leadership of this church was talking about the less privileged people of their community as *others*. Using phrases like "*Those people* don't have enough money to provide for their families." And "*Those people* are in great need." And "*Those people* need our help." They had honorable aspirations and noble intentions, but, unconsciously, this church was communicating, "We do not expect *those people* to be in our church."

But it made me wonder, *Shouldn't those people be the very people the church is built on? Shouldn't the* others *be a valued and integral part of our churches and communities?*

When we turn people into *others*, we begin to believe that justice is about occasionally helping people who are different and then retreating back into our cozy, middle-class churches as we pat ourselves on the backs for being the heroes.

As the God of the universe, Jesus could very well have redeemed the entire human race with a snap of His fingers or the whisper of His voice. He could have sent in someone else to do His dirty work. He could have made a one-day trip down to this planet to be the hero.

If there was anyone who deserved to be the hero, it was Jesus. If there was anyone who deserved to send someone else to do the dirty work, it was Jesus. If there was anyone who deserved to retreat to a palace after a day in the filth of disease, and the sorrow of humanity, and the desperation of loss, and the disdain of the religious, it was Jesus.

But He didn't do any of those things. He "became flesh and blood, and moved into the neighborhood" (John 1:14, MSG). He entered into your story and into mine. He walked the earth, He heard our stories, He touched our pain, and He embraced our messy lives. He was born in a barn to an unwed mother, grew up the son of a carpenter, made friends with the down-and-out, was welcomed into ministry by the crazy desert guy who ate locusts and wore camel skin, gathered a team of picked-over leaders, was run out of town by people who didn't understand Him, was arrested by the government, was beaten and spit on, and was killed next to criminals in the most humiliating and brutal way possible. He lived and died alongside real people, and, as He did, He ushered true and lasting justice into their lives.

Although Jesus is the ultimate Hero of our stories, He didn't act like one. Rather, He asked questions and healed people and then told people not to tell anyone. His healing and justice were strategic, intentional, and long-term. He came to break the chains of systemic injustice, not to swoop in and briefly play the hero.

Jesus came to give Himself away, not to be the hero. And He created you to give yourself away, not to be the hero.

Jesus doesn't see His people in two groups. He doesn't see the privileged as His "helpers" and the less privileged as the "others." He sees people as people. He sees value in every life. He sees world-changing potential in the eyes of every one of His children. No matter our ethnicity or our income level, our gender or our nationality, our immigration status or whether we have a place to call home—Jesus just sees people.

Do we?

WE ARE LOVE

There is something about the wild spirit of the ocean that makes me feel right at home, as though God used the same paintbrush on the ocean as He did on my soul. Today, as the wind whips my cheeks and tousles my hair, the waves are raging and roaring in front of me, a force to be reckoned with, a strength that almost makes me jealous. They curl over themselves and crash into each other as though they are clamoring to get ahead and be the first to reach the shore.

I'm sitting on the sand in the first flash of daylight with my computer in my lap because I'm *that* author. The one who brings her computer to oceans and mountains and airplanes and restaurants because the best experiences bring out the best writing. At least, they do for me. I'm wearing my oversize tropical sweatshirt again because what else would I be wearing? Different seasons call for different uniforms. And I'm not sure why this season seems to call for a loud, crazy, too-big, brightly colored sweatshirt, but it does.

Maybe it's because that's exactly what this season has been. Loud, a lot of crazy, a little too big for what I think I'm qualified for, but full of so much brightness and hope and beauty and goodness and fun and dreams coming to fruition right before my eyes.

And in the midst of it all, as I look out at the clamoring waves, I see my soul in the good and in the bad, in the wild and the free and the whimsical and the loud, but also in the competing and the pushing and the rushing and the roaring. I know, deep down inside, I, too, am competing to be the first one to the shore. I think if I can push just a little bit harder, if I can work just a little bit longer, if I can do just a little bit better, I'll arrive. I'll realize all my grandiose visions and larger-than-life dreams. I'll finally be the hero I always knew I could be.

But I'm not. We're not. And it's time to stop trying to be the hero. Because it just doesn't work.

We won't discover long-term solutions to the human trafficking system while trying to be the hero.

We won't bring systemic change to racist practices and laws while trying to be the hero.

We won't reform the foster care system while trying to be the hero.

We won't empower individuals to break out of a cycle of poverty while trying to be the hero.

We won't usher peace into places of conflict while trying to be the hero.

We won't make any difference in the global refugee crisis while trying to be the hero.

We won't bring any lasting, real, sustainable, systemic change if our entire aim is a singular heroic life.

The fight against injustice in our world isn't a walk-in-the-park kind of fight. This is an all-out, give-everything-you-have, make-deep-sacrifices, get-right-in-the-mess, fall-down-and-get-up kind of fight. And if we're in it for ourselves, we just won't last.

GENERATION DISTINCT

"WE WON'T BRING ANY LASTING,
REAL, SUSTAINABLE, SYSTEMIC
CHANGE IF OUR ENTIRE AIM IS A
SINGULAR HEROIC LIFE."

This fight requires something different, something stronger, something so much deeper.

The injustice of our world is deep, and dark, and oppressive, and wrong. It will make us sob deeply. It will cause us to shake in fear. It will cause us to become sick, to have nightmares, to stare evil right in the face. Being the hero cannot sustain us, keep us in the fight, or give us the perseverance to continue the battle.

We need a motivation that will trump any evil, any hate, any oppression, any wrong, any injustice. Our fight for justice must always come from a deep, holy, radical, dangerous kind of love.

A love that says I'll fight for you.

A love that says you matter.

A love that says I'll put my life in danger to rescue yours.

A love that sacrifices.

A love that moves toward the conflict.

A love that shows up when everyone else leaves.

A love that sees past skin color or nationality or religion or race.

A love that is consistent.

A love that fights for truth.

A love that sees the image of the Creator in every single human being.

A love that always honors all people.

We are *not* the heroes. We are something better: We are love. And love actually changes things.

GOING PAST BARBED WIRE

It hit me as I was rushing through the New York airport for my connecting flight. This fiercely extroverted people person was about to embark on a solitary trip to a country where I didn't know a single soul. I boarded the little plane, blinking quickly to clear my foggy, tear-filled eyes, terrified to embark on this journey alone.

I knew I had to go. I knew it at a soul level. My soul was moving my body toward this opportunity. So often, we find our feet moving, dragging our souls along as they dig their heels into the dirt trying to get some attention. They try to yell, "This isn't what we're really longing for; let us show you what we're searching for." But our bodies and minds roll our eyes at our bold little souls and keep moving forward anyway. And then we realize we never found the purpose we were searching for, and we wonder why. But our souls are still there, wondering if we'll ever give them a chance to share the truth they've known all along.

For one of the first moments of my life, I was finally letting my soul lead. And my wild, fearless soul dragged me all the way to New York—and then my body finally started to speak up again. "What are you doing? You're about to board a plane and go to a country where you don't know a single person. This plan is never going to work. You're going to be all alone. What do you think you're doing?" But still, I pushed my tears aside and stepped onto the plane.

The whole plane ride, I tried to find ways to distract myself. But when the pilot announced we were about to land, all I could do was swallow hard, blink quickly to clear the tears, and put on my bravest face. It was time to enter the unknown adventure before me.

I didn't yet know that there, in the midst of the wooden-plank shacks, dusty roads, starvation, need, and poverty, I would discover the most beautiful, pure friendship I had ever encountered.

Some people may see little beauty in the streets of the village where I found myself. At first glance, it can seem nothing more than a disheartening picture of the poverty and desperation that exists in this world. This town is often avoided or forgotten.

But there is beauty there. I have seen it. I have heard it. I have met it.

I saw it in the smiling eyes of beautiful children. I heard it in their giggles as they chased me around their village. I met it each morning as I walked outside to a chorus of *"Hola, Hannah! Hola, Hannah!"* I tasted it in the meals that families insisted I share with them when they barely had enough food for themselves. I encountered it as I was welcomed into their tents and shacks with a love I didn't feel I deserved. They loved me for no other reason than because I was a person just like them.

I was the only white girl in a village of beautiful Dominican people, teaching at a school, trying my best to speak a language I deeply loved but was far from fluent in—and they welcomed me into their communities and made me feel like I mattered to them. That kind of abundant love is radical.

After a few weeks of being hit by this unconventional kind of love, one of my new friends came up to me after we were done teaching at the school for the day and said, *"Ven conmigo a escalar la montaña!"* And when someone invites me to climb a mountain, I have a strict policy to never, ever say no.

If this book feels less like a book and more like a love letter to mountains, I can't help it. Mountains just seem to be the place where God catches my attention and blows my mind and changes my perspective and shows me Himself over and over and over.

My friend rallied the other young adults who taught at the school, and before we knew it, ten Dominicans and the American were setting off toward the mountain.

We loudly and emphatically bounded toward the base of the mountain, sharing our lives and drinking in the beauty and laughing at the mistakes I made as I spoke their language. This wasn't the kind of mountain climb I was used to. There wasn't a clear, marked trail for us to take. In fact, I don't know if we were allowed to be on that mountain at all. Every time we approached another barbed-wire fence, my Dominican friends smoothly navigated us through—one person used their shirt to cover their hand and lift the top wire up while another person used their shirt to cover their hand and push the bottom wire lower. And one by one, we snuck through the middle.

When we made it to the top, I was infatuated by the view. We hung out at the peak for a while and basked in the glory of the lush jungle scenes . . . until we looked around and realized we had severely miscalculated the time and the sun had already started to set. We gathered our things and quickly began our descent. Only, once again, we weren't taking a path. We were just wandering down the side of a huge mountain in the dark. And this mountain wasn't just rock. It was muddy and slick, causing us to slip most of our way down.

I pride myself on being a good hiker. But I wasn't used to this muddy, no-path, pitch-dark, falling-rocks kind of hiking. And I continued to fall, sliding long distances down the mountain, trying any way I could to secure my footing. Once again, my friends—expert climbers in these conditions—had a plan. They placed one of the strongest guys right in front of me, leading the way, and another right behind me. Whenever I began to slide, the friend behind me would yell to the friend in front of me, who would brace himself to catch me before I slid too far. And if a rock gave way under my feet or I took a misstep in the dark, the friend behind me would grab my arm and keep me from taking a dangerous spill.

All down the mountain, these two young men were literally catching me to make sure I didn't fall. These two young men who didn't speak my language, live in my country, or have the same skin color as mine were pulling me away from danger and protecting me from taking a hit. They didn't owe me anything. I was just some white girl from America who was visiting their country. I was the outsider and the *other*.

Like many of us who go on short-term mission trips, I'd initially arrived expecting to *give* something to the people. But I don't believe I gave anything. Instead, these friends offered me a picture of what it really means to do life together, to support one another in our wild adventures and risky endeavors and dangerous escapades. It doesn't matter if we look different, or come from unique cultures, or have completely different stories, or even speak diverse languages. We link arms with people who just choose to love us enough to say, "I've got you. If you fall, I'll catch you. And I'll walk with you as we get back on the path."

DISAGREEING IN A COFFEE SHOP

I used to think I had to find a tribe of fiercely passionate people who were fighting for justice and creating change and ushering hope into their communities so I could join them in what they were doing. But sometimes we have to create the things we long to be a part of.

This is how the Just Tribe started.

I didn't want to do it when I woke up that Saturday morning. It was a sparkling May morning. Chicago had finally taken its first deep breath of spring. And it felt like my whole corner of the world had breathed a deep sigh of relief. The brown, slushy mush had slowly melted away, and the sun was suddenly more gracious in making itself known. Birds were coming back to the party, warming up their vocal cords for the summer that was to come. The wind was even different that morning—gentle instead of biting. It kindly drifted through the open windows of my car instead of harshly whipping around the corner of every building as I drove toward the first meeting of our Just Tribe.

I showed up early to the coffee shop to save a table. Of course, I didn't know who exactly I was saving seats for because I had no idea who was going to show up. More accurately, I had no idea *if* anyone would show up.

I was in the coffee shop on this bright May morning because I was tired of the approach many Christians were taking to the big, controversial issues in our world—*Don't talk about it. Or, if you do, at least don't talk about it around people who might disagree with you.*

I think our world is bad at disagreeing. We're scared of entering deep conversations with people who think differently than we do. We're afraid of discussing big issues in circles of people who have a variety of ideas and perspectives. And, I think, for far too long the people who claim to love Jesus have been the worst at it.

I couldn't take it any longer. My Twitter feed is inundated with new issues every day. People wage war through their iPhones while refusing to sit down with the people they attack through the safety of a screen. But when I sit down for a cup of coffee with a friend, we stay far away from even slightly hard things—we talk about the weather and how our week is going and whether we're caught up on the latest TV shows and if we've been on any dates recently. Somehow, the conversations that really matter seem to be either destructive or off-limits.

At some point, it became out of line to mention an issue we saw in the news in conversation with the people in our lives. Without even realizing it, we bought into the lie that *it is better to be nice than to wrestle with big issues*—and the lie that *it is easier to pretend we agree on everything than to learn how to love people we disagree with.*

But avoidance doesn't lead to unity. It just leads to greater distance between us as we keep it all together in real life and tear each other apart on social media. Activists don't earn their stripes by participating in a march, or contacting their government to advocate for a change to a law, or rescuing girls off the street, or taking kids into their homes, or feeding the homeless, or welcoming the refugee to their table. Instead, they claim their title by posting bold opinions on social media.

In the middle of all this, my soul was gasping for a fresh breath of truth, a fresh breath of unity, a fresh breath of love. So I texted a group of my friends a really simple message: I would be at my favorite local coffee shop for a couple hours one Saturday morning every month. If they wanted to take the complex conversations off social media and experience them in real life, they should come. If they were dissatisfied with the prevalence of injustice in our world and in our very own communities and they wanted to do something about it, they should come. If they wanted to talk about hard, divisive, polarizing issues in a safe place where we could share opinions and disagree and love one another anyway, they should come. That was it.

I told myself I didn't care how many people showed up. But I did. I wanted a huge mass of people to show up, to feel the same longing I had for new and better ways of connecting, to seek to create a new *lifestyle* of disagreeing and loving one another anyway. But that didn't happen. And, in the end, it was a good thing, a safe and intimate place for wholeness to grow.

On that spring Saturday, a group of five young adults drank coffee and sat around a table and talked about things we had never talked about in real life. We talked about the major issues in our world that were plastered all over our news channels and Twitter feeds and magazines. We talked about different perspectives and different ideas and different opinions.

And do you know what? We even disagreed. And it was beautiful and sacred and right. We got better. We stretched our minds. We heard new ideas and learned from unique perspectives. We took a posture of humility and didn't claim to have everything figured out. We looked at the life of Jesus and based our ideas on what He taught. We spoke boldly for truth and extended grace because we're all still on the journey.

At the end of the conversation, one of my friends spoke up. In a holy moment, he said something that would forever change the meaning of unity for me: "I think all of this, this entire conversation, isn't really about justice. I think it's actually about honor."

That's what it means to build unity. It means we honor the image of God that lies within every single person.

So now, the Just Tribe is part of a lifestyle for me and a handful of people. Sometimes a whole group shows up, and sometimes just one friend sits across from me. Every single time, my heart expands. Every single time, I hear a new perspective that opens my eyes and causes me to see people, all people, just a little more as God intended.

I don't think our world is full of tension and conflict and disunity because we really hate each other. I think we just don't know each other. And I think we're afraid of what we don't know. And I think we're afraid to admit that we don't know what we don't know.

But Jesus didn't live like that. Yes, Jesus disagreed with the Pharisees—but He went exactly to where He knew they would be and had real conversations with them. If there was anyone who surely didn't need to listen to the opinions of others, the Creator of the universe would probably be off the hook. But Jesus Himself entered their lives, and He asked them questions, and He shared truth. He even became angry. He called them out. And He listened.

Friends, if we ever want to witness our world come together in unity, we must build communities of God's wildly diverse people. What if our tribes were a mosaic of lives, stories, perspectives, backgrounds, opinions, ideas, and cultures? What if we sat around the table with people who have different opinions and who may even push up against some of our tightly held opinions—and we chose to honor the image of God that lies within them?

So, where's your table? Who are the people filling those chairs? Who are you disagreeing with? Who are you learning from? Who are you processing with? And do they think just like you? Do they look just like you? Do they believe exactly what you believe? Let's choose to expand our perspective, pull up a chair at our table for more voices, and honor each other *as* we wrestle with big ideas and challenge each other—and even as we disagree. We all benefit when we choose to invite more voices to the table.

If we, as the next generation, create tribes that aren't based on how similar we are but on how different we are, we would find ourselves remaking the world. Walls of racism, hate, sexism, judgment, and fear would be torn down. And maybe, just maybe, hope would crash into our world, and everything would change, and a whole new generation of people who choose love over hate would lead us into a brand-new kind of future.

I want to be a part of that kind of tribe. Don't you?

We are better when we are united.

We are stronger when we are diverse.

We are bolder when we link arms.

"WE ARE BETTER WHEN WE ARE UNITED. WE ARE STRONGER WHEN WE ARE DIVERSE. WE ARE BOLDER WHEN WE LINK ARMS."

BUILD YOUR TRIBE

All of your favorite stories have at least one thing in common. It's more than your favorite actor, genre, or series. There is something about the best stories that remind us of what is possible, that infuse us with hope, that surround us with vision for our own lives. Your favorite movies and TV shows and books all boast a common theme.

There is a tribe of people who are all working together toward a common goal.

Because the souls of humanity call out for people. We're designed for people. We're created for people. We thrive the most when we have people. So if we know we are so deeply in need of a tribe, why don't we take the steps to create it?

It's as though we know in principle that we need people. But we don't know how to put action behind those needs. So we just wait, hoping one day someone will invite us into their community, or we'll just magically stumble on the perfect tribe. And when that doesn't happen, we retreat further within ourselves and become isolated and discouraged and alone. But this is no way to live our lives. In fact, we were never created to live our lives that way.

But here is what happens. You get home from college, or you arrive home after a service trip, or you find yourself back in your hometown after a retreat where you experienced real, authentic, powerful, unified community. You say, "Hannah, I know what it feels like to do life with a tribe because I've experienced it."

And I say, "You're right." But often tribes are given to us in programs. And when we experience them in a program, we begin to believe it's normal for these tribes to exist in everyday life, too. So we leave college, enter the world of jobs and apartments and church-hunting, and are confused when we don't have a group of people around us all the time. We get home from the service trip, go back to work, and wonder why no one else seems to care about poverty the way our tribe did. We walk off the plane after an incredible retreat and can't figure out why, instead of feeling filled up and excited, we feel sad and lonely.

It's because the real world isn't college and it isn't a trip and it isn't a program. In the real world, we might have small groups, or coworkers, or friends, or people we do stuff with because we don't want to sit at home alone every night. But we would never consider these people our tribe. We find ourselves saying things like "I'll just never have community like I did in college." Or "I can't even explain to you how close our team became on that trip." Or "I need to reconnect with the people from that program because I've never experienced friendship like that."

Without even realizing it, we have resigned

ourselves to never experiencing a deep tribe again. So we wistfully look back to the people we had before.

But this is no way to live. We were never created for loneliness.

I do not believe a tribe is something we should only experience in a program. The opportunity to do life within a group of people who are unafraid to be with you and for you and go deep is one of the most beautiful, sacred gifts God has given to us. And if that's the case, then it makes sense we should do everything we can to build that tribe instead of just waiting for it to happen.

It is not someone else's responsibility to fill the cravings of our souls. It is not our church's responsibility, or our family's responsibility, or our mentor's responsibility, or our friends' responsibility. It is *our* responsibility to do the things that set our souls on fire. It is *our* responsibility to seek out the things our souls crave. It is *our* responsibility to do the hard work and invest the time and pour ourselves out to create the very things we are searching for.

So start a Just Tribe. Or join a club on campus. Have a conversation with the person you see every morning at the gym. Ask the person sitting next to you in church to grab a cup of coffee. Join an adult sports league in your city. Reach out to that person on Instagram who lives in your city and has the same passions as you. Volunteer for a local nonprofit. Start a cohort with some people you know where you read leadership books and get together to share what you're learning. Gather friends together to take a deep dive into the Bible. Invite a group of people to invest in at-risk kids in your community together. Text some friends, inviting them to run a race with you to raise money for a cause you really believe in. Gather a group of friends to help you create an event in your community to love on foster kids in your city. Grab some buddies and intentionally care for a refugee family in your area. Ask some friends to create something with you that inspires the world—a documentary, a vlog, a book, an album, an initiative, a business.

Take whatever you love and combine it with your love for Jesus; then invite some people to join you to create real change in the world.

When Jesus began His ministry, He invited a tribe to join Him. He chose twelve people. He could have done it alone. But even the Son of God knew there was value in doing life, changing the world, and starting a movement alongside a tribe of people. He didn't wait until they came to Him. He went out and invited them. I think we are so afraid of rejection that we never build deep friendships or invite people into our lives. But don't let that stop you. The tribe you have been searching for, yearning for, and desperately seeking after could very well be on the other side of your step of bravery.

So send that text.

Have that conversation.

Gather those people.

Send that email.

Right now. Put the book down, and go do something that could transform your life.

You were created for a tribe. So go out and create your own.

THE WILDEST KINDS OF LOVE

The snow was relentless. As is Chicago's style, we found ourselves in the midst of another whiteout storm. Streets were icy and slushy. People were staying in their homes, cozied around their fireplaces, enjoying the after-Christmas lull. It was December 28, and most people were in their sweatpants, still snacking on leftover holiday ham and brightly colored Christmas cookies. The weather channel told us to keep inside. The radio stations urged us to settle in, get comfortable, stay warm. But my friends and I had something else in mind. We weren't about to let the danger keep us indoors. We had some work to do. We had some dreams to build. We had a future to create.

We didn't know what we were doing. We didn't know we needed a business plan or a mission statement or bylaws or a budget. We just knew we wanted to empower young leaders, change the world, and build a better future. So we started anyway.

We had an idea to capture fifty-two videos of fifty-two people presenting fifty-two different ways to create an impact. Every Monday, we'd release a new video and challenge young adults to get off the sidelines and start living lives that mattered.

We had only launched a few months earlier. And when I say "launched," what I really mean is we bought a domain name, made a website, and told people we had launched.

We had invited twenty-five people to join us for that first video shoot. We had twenty-five scripts written. We had twenty-five challenges prepared. The only thing we didn't have was a place to shoot the video. We looked at every option. Well, every *free* option. We looked and looked and looked. With the day of the video shoot fast approaching, we still didn't have a location. Finally, one of my fellow dreamers mentioned that her dad had generously offered for us to use an available building of his.

We didn't ask many questions about the space. We were desperate. And it was free. He said yes, and we were thrilled. We had our space, we had our people, and we had our vision. We were ready for whatever would come our way. At least, we thought we were.

But when we showed up that day in December, we were not prepared for what we were about to experience. I pulled up and thought I must be in the wrong place. There was no large warehouse, no cozy office space, no empty storefront. Just a big abandoned building with a cracked and dirty sign out front that read, "Monkey Joe's."

Now, for those of you who haven't gotten to experience the crazy-loud wildness of Monkey Joe's, it's an indoor amusement park created to bring joy to children and terror to their parents. It was not what I had envisioned for our new organization's video shoot.

I zipped up my coat and shoved a hat onto my head, then ran toward the entrance to the building. When I opened the door, I was ready to breathe a sigh of relief at the warmth. There are a lot of words I could use to describe the space. But *warm* was not one of them. I looked around at the dark interior. "Alex!" I called out to my friend who had gotten there before me. "Why is it so . . . cold?"

Her loud laugh echoed off the cold cement as she emerged from a back hallway. "Well . . . I guess they turned the heat off."

I looked at her with a blank stare as the snow-flakes melted on my head and dripped down onto my shoulders. "It's not going to get any warmer in here?" I guess I thought if I asked the question differently, I might get a response I liked more.

"Nope. This is it," she said.

I winced and started to laugh. "I hope our friends dress warmly." I shook my head. And that was only the beginning.

As we wandered around the enormous space, trying to find the perfect spot to shoot our videos, we stepped over broken glass bottles and tripped over large pipes. All we had was a camera—we didn't even have a tripod to put the camera *on*. So we found crates and boxes and stacked them all on top of each other and set the camera on top. We wound lights around wooden pallets and called it a "video set."

One by one, our people began to show up. The sweetest, kindest, most loyal friends in the world drove through a snowstorm on dangerously icy streets to gather in a dirty, freezing, creepy warehouse to spend hours shooting videos because we shared the same crazy dream.

And you know what? In the midst of it all, we were living lives that mattered. We were giving ourselves to a vision greater than ourselves. We were making sacrifices to build a better future. We were investing our time in something that would make a difference.

If I'd been there by myself in that old Monkey Joe's, the day would have been completely different. I wouldn't have found the unexpected cold hilarious. I wouldn't have had people to laugh with about the dust and grime that covered us by the end of the day.

No one would have been there to share the incredible moment when we finally captured the perfect words on camera. Without the community around me, the day wouldn't have been as close to beautiful.

We were linking arms, choosing unity, showing up for each other. We were creating things. We were fighting for change. We were investing in things that matter. We were rallying around a vision. We were uniting around a cause greater than ourselves.

This is why we need tribes. This is why we need our people. Creating change is hard. Building things that last costs us greatly. Fighting for a vision larger than ourselves is scary. But when we do it with a tribe, the hard looks a little more fun, the costs seem just a little lighter, and the vision seems a little less scary. We laugh more. We accomplish more. We hold each other up because we truly are stronger together. When I begin to doubt my ability to lead, my friends remind me who I am. When I feel like I'm drowning in the workload, my team shares the burden. When I need to know I'm not alone, my tribe shows up. When I feel afraid, my people infuse me with courage.

We were never designed to do great work in this world on our own. We were formed for unity. We were created to link arms. We were handcrafted with a longing to belong.

Don't wait for someone else to create the community you long to be a part of. Do it yourself. Don't wait for someone else to invite you to the table. Build a table of your own, and invite as many people as you can to join. Don't wait for a better time to link arms and cross divides and invest in unity. The time is now, and the person is you.

Find your people. Build a tribe. Link arms with others. Life is so much more magical and meaningful when you are surrounded by a tribe of people who are characterized by all the crazy and wildest kinds of love.

MOVEMENT #4

LIVE DISTINCT

Build the Future

*The path for us to follow has already been written.
My time is gone. Yours is still to come.*

I'M GUESSING YOU'VE NEVER HEARD that quote before. You won't find it in an old book or see it carved on an ancient building. It didn't come from the mouth of a great communicator, and it isn't pasted in a frame on the wall of your friend's apartment. I discovered these words in the last place I thought I would find myself.

It was a crisp morning in Pennsylvania when my friends and I slowly walked down a winding gravel path, our breath visible in the cool October air. The sky was gray, but the thick line of blue mountains painting the horizon surrounded us on every side. And the world was quiet. Silent, actually. Not a peep. Only the patter of our boots on soft, damp ground broke the silence as four girls in their twenties explored an unexpected place. We pushed open a metal gate, and it creaked its welcome.

We slowly wound around the tombstones, reading the names and life spans of the people who were buried in this graveyard.

This was not a graveyard where famous people were buried. There were no glamorous names or glamorous pasts. But as we leaned down and read the names of real people, we began to discover their stories. War heroes who lived to be only seventeen years old. Husbands and wives, buried side by side. Children who were laid in the ground before their parents were gray. Priests and pastors. Lawyers and farmers. People. People who had lives and stories and dreams and hopes. People who had families and friends and enemies and lovers.

The graveyard was expansive, rolling over the hills as far as my eyes could see. The wind began to whip harshly, turning our cheeks red, but we couldn't stop wandering and reading. Four young women, all with hopes and dreams and plans, standing in the middle of a sea of completed stories.

Our time there could have felt sad, or even slightly morbid. Instead, it felt beautiful. We were stepping into stories and history and moments lost in time. We noticed silly nicknames engraved on tombstones, brightly colored flowers, and endearing quotes.

And then, as I neared the back corner of the graveyard, I found myself standing in front of the grave of a priest who had lived in the early 1900s. The stone did not say very much about his life.

But reading the quote etched into the gray marble at my feet froze me in the moment: *The path for us to follow has already been written. My time is gone. Yours is still to come.*

This man would never have been featured on the front of *Time* magazine. More than likely, his life wasn't chronicled in a book. There were no records of his voice ever gathering a crowd from around the globe. I had no way to know what he looked like or to learn about all the ways he made a difference. He was just a man buried in the back corner of a cold, damp graveyard in a little mountain town in the woods of Pennsylvania. And yet, his words changed me.

My time is gone. Yours is still to come.

Even in his death, he is issuing you and me an invitation to live a life that matters. To live a grander story. To say yes, even when we are afraid. To say no to injustice. To jump into the unknown. To risk and explore and pour ourselves out to build a better future for the generations to come.

We are not on a mission to make ourselves look great. We are not on a mission to live incredible lives. We are not on a mission to start a movement that ends when we die.

In that cold mountain air, on an ordinary Friday, in a remote town in Pennsylvania, I was reminded that one day, we will come to the end of our lives— and it will be our turn to pass the baton to those who follow us. Today, that baton is in your hand.

What will you do with it?

DO THE THING

I was shaken awake at 3:30 a.m. "Wake up, Hannah. It's time."

I grudgingly rolled out of bed and stumbled into the bathroom. I was only half-awake as I washed my face and brushed my teeth. I grabbed my hat and backpack and walked up the stairs.

"Now do I get to know where we're going?" I asked. Faith shook her head, and we got in the car and began to drive. We passed familiar sights, zooming down the Chicago highway in the pitch black of an early spring morning.

Suddenly we got off the highway, and I knew exactly where we were going.

"Why are we going to the airport?" I demanded. Faith just smiled.

We pulled up to O'Hare and I followed her out of the car with nothing but my backpack. She walked right inside and turned around to look at me. I had no idea what to think. "I have meetings tomorrow," I told her.

She laughed, pulled two tickets out of her bag, and gave them to me. I scanned the ticket quickly, and my gaze snagged on *LaGuardia Airport*. I looked up at her, *What the heck?* written all over my face.

"We are flying," she said, "to spend thirteen hours in New York."

And that is exactly what we did. We hopped on a plane and arrived in New York City to fill thirteen hours with as many memories as possible.

We wandered around Times Square and walked across the Brooklyn Bridge. We had our caricatures drawn in Central Park and found the sweetest little tea shop in the city and ate hot dogs from a cart. By the time we collapsed onto the plane just thirteen hours later, our bodies were weary, but our spirits were wildly awake.

There is something about that kind of life that I love. A life of spontaneous moments. A story that shakes you awake and invites you into adventures you never saw coming. A story that leads you to unexpected places at unexpected times.

I meet with young people every single week who have resigned themselves to a smaller vision than the life they were created for. They're saying yes to things that don't matter because they're waiting for a better time to say yes to the things that do matter.

Friends—I'm afraid we're not living like our lives will echo in eternity. We can pretend we are. We can tell each other we are. We can post on social media like we are. But we're not. At least, I'm often not.

We don't need more money or time or permission. We just need to say yes. It's up to us.

Small yeses turn into big yeses. We don't have to know the whole story when we begin writing the first chapter. Our generation is at risk of missing writing the big story altogether because we're so worried we'll start the first chapter wrong. But we don't have any guarantees for how long we get to be on this planet.

So let's stop waiting for some moment in the future. Let's grab our pen and start writing.

Let's send the email,
make the phone call,
walk across the street,
quit the job,
fill out the application,
get on the plane,
write the song,
open the business,
start the initiative,
raise the money,
run the race,
sponsor the child,
mentor the student,
preach the message,
schedule the meeting.
Let's just do the thing we say we'll do eventually.

Because life is happening right now all around us, in all of its intoxicating beauty and whimsy and unpredictability.

So let's just do the thing. Let's build the lives we want to live. Let's mold existences we fall in love with over and over and over. Let's write stories we love to read.

The entire world is open to us—if we will only say yes.

Your life is not happening to you. You are happening to your life. So many of us are living like the greatest call on our lives is self-preservation, so we don't put ourselves in positions to feel afraid, or unsure, or uncomfortable, or stretched, or exhausted, or embarrassed, or in over our heads.

But, more often than not, that is exactly what a life that changes the world looks like. Every single one of my heroes has built a life centered on the very things we run so far away from. Because living a life that matters doesn't happen in the convenient life, or the comfortable life, or the easy life, or the safe life, or the perfectly scheduled life, or the ordinary life. It happens right smack-dab in the middle of the hard, difficult, scary, dangerous, risky, uncomfortable, interruptible, sacrificial, abnormal life. So let's stop looking around at our culture to discover how we should live. Let's build a different kind of life.

If we want to see real change in our world, we must

"YOUR LIFE IS NOT HAPPENING
TO YOU. YOU ARE HAPPENING
TO YOUR LIFE."

take seriously the responsibility of carrying this baton. It's a sacred honor. It's a deep privilege. We are alive at this point of history for this very moment. Will we waste the time we have just holding this baton? Or will we carry it further than ever before? If change starts with us, then we need to become leaders who build a better future.

Becoming the very best leaders we can be may just be the least selfish ambition we ever commit to. This pursuit of growth will not be for ourselves; this pursuit of growth will be born out of a desperate desire to build a better future for the generations to come.

How do we get there? We have to get serious, do the hard work, and build this life. And we must lay four core bricks as our foundation:

1. Investing
2. Learning
3. Fighting
4. Thriving

BRICK 1: INVESTING

If you asked me who I was investing in, I would tell you about the high school girls I have invested in since they were in fifth and sixth grade. These girls have deep access to my life. I'm "on call" in their lives. And they trust me in those moments because I have shown up time after time after time.

Together, we've wrestled through pain and heartache and trauma and loss. And together we've walked through the band concerts, basketball games, graduations, birthdays, summer camps, and quinceañeras. In the devastating sorrow and the big events of life and the ordinary moments in between, we've been together. Because when we show up for the little moments, we can trust each other to show up for the big ones.

Investing in others is a part of our lives we can't outsource. We can't use an app, hire an assistant, or develop a system. We have to schedule real time in our calendars to get out of our own heads and invest in someone else.

I do this because I want to invest in the next generation of women who will be leading churches, families, culture, and the world. I want them to know Jesus. I mean really, really know Jesus. And if God wants to use me in their journey toward Jesus, then I'm going to say yes.

And, truly, this is one of the best parts of my life.

When I doubt that I am making any difference in the world, when I feel overwhelmed by the demands of leadership, when I wonder if my life really matters, God reminds me of my girls.

He reminds me of the moments spent sitting in circles as they share things they haven't told a single soul. The exhaustion of holding in those secrets begins to fade from their eyes, and I see a flash of hope. I hold their hands and give them space to weep. And my girls surround one another with embraces and love and kindness and support. I see the power of what happens when we unite instead of compete.

Those of us around the circle really don't have much in common. In fact, we couldn't be more different. There are Muslims and atheists and Christians of different denominations and those undecided about spirituality in general. There are cheerleaders and basketball players and flautists. One is even an Olympic powerlifter. We're different races; we come from different backgrounds; we have different opinions, viewpoints, beliefs, and positions. We live with different family dynamics and cultural traditions.

And yet, in the moments of crisis and fear and sorrow and pain, we see past what makes us different and instead see what makes us the same. The love we experience together as we surround and support one another has marked me forever. I love better because I have watched these young women love so beautifully. I have seen girls understand who Jesus is for the very first time as the sun rises and splashes through coffee shop windows, flashing red and pink and orange light on our faces. I have watched them break free from addictions. I have shed tears alongside them as they showed me scars on their wrists. I have witnessed them dive deep into the big questions of their faith.

We've shared laughter and celebrated their victories—and we've wept and mourned their losses. I have held their hands as they wondered if life was still worth living. I have been blown away by their courage as they boldly led other people to know Jesus. I have been inspired by them as they stepped up to take the baton to lead their own group of elementary girls. And I have sat back, shaking my head, learning things about Jesus I never knew because of their fearlessness and vulnerability.

We share everyday life together, and, for better or worse, they get to watch the way I choose to live. I pick them up and take them to go on an adventure or invest in our community or join me at a speaking engagement or simply run errands. Sometimes we're rock climbing or hiking along cliffs or jumping into ice-cold lakes. And other times we're just strolling through the grocery store or eating frozen yogurt. We blast the music way too loud and we talk about their friends or their newest crush and we laugh until we cry. They tell me about their dreams and their hopes and their visions and their ideas.

All of it—the beauty and the pain and the sorrow and the laughter and the tears and the celebrations—makes up some of the best parts of my life. Not because it's always easy. Not because it's always fun. But because it always matters. And doing things that matter brings so much more joy, so much more fulfillment, so much more purpose than anything else the world has to offer.

Throughout Jesus' life, we see Him intentionally creating room in His life to invest in others, to bring people along with Him, and to allow them access to His life. And He had the most important mission in all of history. If the Savior of the world had time to invest in others, maybe we do too. This doesn't have to mean adding anything to our lives. In fact, inviting people into our lives and joining them in theirs is the most authentic way to invest. And it may just be the most important thing we do.

If you run, invite someone to run with you. If you box, invite someone to box with you. If you bring your kids to the park, invite someone to go to the park with you. If you go to the grocery store, invite someone to go grocery shopping with you. If you hike, invite someone to hike with you. If you paint, invite someone to paint with you. If you go to the gym, invite someone to work out with you. If you hang out in coffee shops, invite someone to meet you there. Our lives are not our own. They are gifts, offerings that we give back to God, saying, "Use me to walk with people as they journey closer to Your heart."

Who are the people you are investing your life in? Who has deep access to your life? Who will say their journey has been radically different because you showed up in their story? Send an invite, schedule a coffee date, invest in a life. Watching Jesus transform a life through your faithfulness and consistency and intentional love may prove the greatest adventure you ever embark on.

BRICK 2: LEARNING

I wish I could introduce you to all the men and women who have been a part of my story. Men and women who have made sacrifices, made room, made time, and made space for me. People who have inspired me, challenged me, loved me, welcomed me into their families and kitchens and grocery runs and projects and adventures and offices and teams and hikes and ministries and trips and lives.

Some of them have met with me once, and some of them have spent hours and hours of their lives with me. Some of them know they were mentors in my life and some of them don't. But each of them showed me a glimpse of the person I wanted to be and took me on a journey to become that person.

They didn't *have* to welcome me into their lives. And they didn't *have* to care about mine. But they did. And they do. And because of them, my life will never be the same.

We will never become the people we want to be on our own. We will never live lives that matter without reaching out a hand and asking people to bring us along. But don't expect it to come easy. It is not someone else's responsibility to see you grow. It is *your* responsibility to grow. So take ownership.

Who are you learning from? I don't mean who are your teachers, or your pastor, or your small-group leader. I mean who has given you access to their life, allowing you to observe and learn from them? Who are you modeling your life after? When you have a big question you are wrestling with, whom do you ask?

Maybe there's a leader in your community who you respect, and you want to schedule a meeting with her. Maybe you know a man who is an incredible husband, and you want to learn from his journey. Maybe there is a pastor who is truly creating change in the community, and you want to know how. Maybe there is an author whose writing has changed your life, and you need to ask him questions. Maybe there is a chef who is renowned for her work—or a poet or a dancer or a playwright or a parent or a lawyer or a surgeon or a surfer or an activist or a communicator or a musician—and you need to schedule a call or set up an email interview or even fly across the country to meet with them.

Don't show up at that meeting with a pitch or a deal. Show up in a posture of listening. Bring a list of questions. Arrive ready to learn.

I think it's time for us to become serious about the growth we're longing to experience, to spend time around the people who show us a glimpse of who we hope to become. It's time to stop waiting for a better moment. So just ask the question. Schedule the meeting. Send the text. Call the office. Do the thing. Take the next step. You may never know all that lies on the other side of that ask.

BRICK 3: FIGHTING

I used to think that if I read books about injustice, posted on social media about injustice, and inspired other people to fight against injustice, then I could check the box and tell people I was "passionate about social justice." But when I paused to look at my life, I was devastated at what I found.

Nothing about my life told the story of a woman who was passionate about social justice. Nothing about my schedule showed evidence I was a part of creating solutions to the world's deepest needs. Nothing about my bank account proved I cared enough to make sacrifices that actually *cost* me something. Nothing about my routines was centered around spending time with the ostracized or oppressed or forgotten.

My life was relatively normal. I volunteered at my church and went on a few mission trips, and I was even mentoring a handful of young women. And those are all good things. But that didn't mean I was doing anything about fighting for justice. Because I wasn't.

I can still remember the moment. I sat in a room

of people like me in a comfortable auditorium while my heart shattered into a million pieces. I was struck by the horror that millions in our world experience as they flee their homes under the title of refugee.

As the speakers continued to share the devastating stories and overwhelming statistics, I discovered something that would change my approach to fighting injustice forever. These were not just stories. These were not just statistics. These speakers were telling stories about real people. About their friends. About mothers and fathers and sisters and friends and girlfriends and husbands and grandfathers and teachers and doctors. Every one of the stories represented a real person with a real life dealing with the real pain of persecution and violence and terror. These were actual individuals who were fleeing their countries and leaving their homes with no idea if they would ever have the chance to return. They were leaving behind family members and communities and hometowns. These people had hopes and dreams and aspirations just like me but were living a life I could never imagine.

I knew I had to do something. I couldn't be one more person who heard about injustice, shook her head, wiped a tear off her cheek, and went back to Starbucks. I had to do something.

But as we've discussed before, fighting this kind of injustice doesn't require getting on a plane and visiting a refugee camp or traveling around Syria or doing something big and flashy. It turned out I could send an email and start volunteering with an organization that serves refugees right here in my own community. I didn't have a lot of resources or expertise or solutions. But I had a little time, and I had a lot of myself. And sometimes, that is all that's required to fight for justice in the world.

As I created relationships with the refugee families in an apartment complex near my house, it didn't feel like I was doing anything all that important. But I wanted the families I interacted with to know, without a shadow of a doubt, that a girl named Hannah was so glad *they* were part of her community. And that whenever they had an issue or a fear or a concern, I could translate or partner with them or watch their kids or show up when they needed an extra hand. I wanted them to know they were loved. I wasn't necessarily fixing the issue; I didn't need to. But I was doing my part, and that was beautiful.

So what is *your* part? Have you convinced yourself that you're off the hook from fighting injustice because you do a lot of other "Christian" things? Have you told yourself that if you're the best volunteer at your church, you have permission to ignore the homeless families lining your streets? Have you believed the lie that you're too busy hanging out with your small group of people who love Jesus to take any time to invest in young men who are caught in a cycle of drug dealing and poverty? Have you just accepted the fact that work keeps you too busy to start walking down the streets of your city, meeting girls caught in human trafficking?

Because it's time to call out the lie. It's time to reject that false narrative. It's time to follow Jesus, even when that path leads us right into the center of messy, scary, painful injustice.

Friends—this isn't an extra activity or an if-we-have-time invitation. We *must* defend, we *must* speak, we *must* fight for justice for every person until justice is achieved for all. Let's mourn the injustice in our world. Let's grieve the pain. But we *cannot* stop there. We must be compelled to get *off* the sidelines and advocate for justice for every person.

Every. Single. Person.

Let's stop making excuses. If we want to know God, then let's stop ignoring the very thing He said would lead to our deepest understanding of His heart:

- Doing what is just and right
- Rescuing the oppressed
- Standing with the foreigner
- Loving the fatherless
- Caring for the widow
- Defending the cause of the poor and needy[1]

BRICK 4: THRIVING

My 1998 Jeep Cherokee is a slightly beaten-up adventure vehicle. It isn't anything beautiful or fancy. In fact, sometimes it doesn't start. The ceiling is littered with the signatures and doodles of my people, and the radio adds a static effect to my favorite music station.

But when I drive in it, I feel like I am experiencing a story. I wonder who drove it before I did. I wonder what faraway places this Jeep has been. I wonder what stories this Jeep has witnessed. Has it watched the early days of young love? Has it gone off-roading in the mountains? Has it fostered friendship and laughter? Has it carried families across the country?

I imagine it has thousands of stories to tell. That's why I love it. I love feeling like I am a part of a narrative that has been going on for years, and I am just one chapter of the grand story. We were created to be drawn to great stories.

I love many of the names for God. I love that He is my Father, my Redeemer, my Shelter, my Shepherd. But one of my favorite descriptions of God is "Author" (Hebrews 12:2, KJV). I love picturing Him writing, crafting, designing, and poring over my story. I love imagining the moment He decided where I would live, who my parents would be, what I would be good at, the color of my eyes, who my best friend would be, where I would travel, what my laugh would sound like, what I would dream about, what would make me jump for excitement, which foods I would love, the places I would explore, and who I would want around me on the day I breathe my last breath.

I think when I get to heaven, I will sit down with God and say, "You are brilliant! I can't believe the way you crafted my story. There were so many crazy turns, so many plot twists, so many times you were patient with me, so many unexpected joys, so many difficult seasons, so many fun times that led me *here* to Your side. What a beautiful story You wrote."

And I love imagining Him looking back at me and saying, "Thanks for saying yes. You lived a beautiful story that magnified My name."

We often hear the stories of incredible men and women who were called to enter prolonged seasons of waiting with little clarity and no apparent purpose. We read these stories and tell our friends, "Keep waiting. All in God's timing. If you're waiting, you're in good company." And that is true.

Abraham waited for a hundred years to have a son. Moses waited in the desert for forty years before God spoke to him through the burning bush. The disciples were told to wait in Jerusalem until the Holy Spirit came to them. Paul was left waiting for freedom in a prison cell.

These people waited with astonishing courage and incredible tenacity. Waiting is important and holy and sacred and beautiful. But waiting is not the end of the story. The Bible is not just a book about people who waited. It is a wild narrative, full of dramatic stories of people with extraordinary bravery, people who took action even when they didn't have the full picture.

Esther didn't wait for someone else to stand up for her people. She didn't create a pros-and-cons list to decide what to do. She chose to stand before the king. She took action.

Joshua didn't laugh at God when he was asked to walk around the walls of Jericho. He didn't schedule a meeting with his mentor or pray about it for three years. He just heard the voice of God and started walking. He took action.

David didn't read a stack of books about how to operate a slingshot when he heard the threats of Goliath. He didn't pass the job on to someone who appeared more qualified.

He just said yes to God and grabbed five smooth stones. He took action.

Sometimes we are called to wait. And that is good and right. And sometimes we need to take time to pray, to reflect, and to pursue the wisdom of trusted voices in our lives. But is it possible for us to absorb the stories of waiting so deeply into our souls that we assume we will always be called to wait?

Maybe, sometimes, we just need to act. Maybe we just need to take the step. Maybe we need to stop waiting for a sign to appear in the sky and just do the thing we know we were born to do. Sometimes we need to say yes to the grander story God longs to write in our lives.

You know you have a passion for women to be empowered in places where they have no access to education, but you haven't started using your skills to provide a solution.

You know you have a passion to love on high schoolers, but you haven't started serving in student ministry because you're waiting for a less busy season.

You know you have a passion to advocate for unity and justice in the face of racism, but you haven't reached across divides to create relationships with people who look different from you.

You know you have a passion to see children find safe homes, but you haven't welcomed a child from the foster care system into your own home.

You know you have a passion to invest in young men growing up without fathers, but you haven't ever taken the time to meet with them.

When we're perpetually waiting, we're not thriving. We're caught in the "one day" cycle. We say we'll do it "one day." But years go by, and the "one day" dream becomes this crazy idea we had when we were younger, not a reality that could affect countless lives.

What are you putting off with the excuse of waiting? What if the ideas, plans, hopes, and dreams we have within us aren't mistakes or something that will happen when we think we're "ready"? What if, instead, they are glimpses of the person God has created us to be and the story He has called us to live?

What if God is handing us wild ideas, big plans, remarkable hopes, and imaginative dreams and is waiting to see what we will do with everything He's placed within us? What if our ideas could change our culture? What if our plans could transform lives? What if our hopes could inspire the people around us? What if our dreams could usher justice into our world?

Your life is not just about existing. Your story is not just about surviving. You are invited to discover the things in this world that set your heart and soul on fire. You are invited to thrive. You are invited to build a life that matters. But it isn't someone else's responsibility to do this. It's yours. It's mine. It's ours together.

LET'S KEEP GOING

Day after day, I sit in coffee shops across from bright, brilliant, beautiful people who feel overwhelmed, overbusy, and overcommitted. And yet, at the very same time, they feel stagnant, stuck, purposeless, lonely, bored, unchallenged, and completely void of passion or meaning. They say something I have heard so very many times from people of all seasons and places and ages: "There has to be more for me than this life I'm living."

I listen and I nod my head. I give them space to process and to express the stirrings and longings that lie deep in their souls. Then I ask some simple questions.

"How are you investing in others?"

They respond that they're trying to invest . . . but they're too busy, so they just stopped volunteering in student ministry or mentoring that young man or volunteering with the nonprofit in their community. "It's *too much*."

I keep going. "Who are the people you are learning from?"

They tell me they wish someone would mentor them, but no one has offered. "I just don't know if I have the space to really invest well in a mentoring relationship in this season."

Then I ask, "Well, how are you fighting for justice?"

They respond that they wish they had space and time to fight for justice, but it all just seems overwhelming with the to-do list that is never completed. "I don't have the margin."

Finally, I say, "What are you doing that makes your soul come alive?"

And they look back at me with a blank stare. They tell me how they wish they could spend time doing the things they love, but work or school or life just feels too busy. "Once I finish this season, I'll have more time."

I realize they don't want answers. They want to be told the very same thing every other person they have met with has told them: "It sounds like you need some rest."

But I don't say that. And we find ourselves sitting in an awkward silence because they're expecting me to say something I'm not going to say.

We live in an age of paradox. Rest is preached and taught everywhere we go, from the pulpit to the coffee shop to the blogs to the bookstore. Everywhere we look, rest is celebrated as important and good and right.

And yet we also are witnessing more burnout, more mental health struggles, and more suicide than ever before. People aren't resting. They're going a million miles a minute, searching for anything they can find that will give them a quick thrill, or a hint of happiness, or a flash of contentment.

I know I've been a victim of this epidemic. I've experienced intense burnout. I've felt the emptiness, the fatigue, the loneliness, the fear, the desperation. It's dangerous, and it's threatening more people than ever before.

But I don't think the answer is to stop everything we're doing that matters. I don't think the answer is to quit serving, quit investing, quit fighting for justice—and just sit at home with a warm cup of tea and an afghan and "rest." At least, I can't find that anywhere in the Bible.

So, what is the answer?

No one so poetically, so beautifully, so delicately, or so boldly described the fullness of rest as Jesus Himself:

"Are you tired? Worn out? Burned out on religion? Come to me. Get away with me and you'll recover your life. I'll show you how to take a real rest. Walk with me and work with me—watch how I do it. Learn the unforced rhythms of grace. I won't lay anything heavy or ill-fitting on you. Keep company with me and you'll learn to live freely and lightly."

MATTHEW 11:28-30, MSG

His words are beautiful and inspiring, deeply challenging and deeply difficult. But I wonder if our generation has heard it so many times, we have grown numb to the gravity of His warning.

In all of this talk about rest, we're missing the central reason why Jesus was so insistent His disciples engage in this practice. It wasn't because their college courses were giving them too much homework. It wasn't because their to-do list was too long. It wasn't because their kids had too many after-school programs. It wasn't because they had scheduled too many coffee dates with friends that week. It wasn't because their work deadlines were closing in. It wasn't because they had too many church events to attend. It wasn't because they had stayed out too late partying on the weekend. It wasn't because they had volunteered for too many Sundays in a row. It wasn't because they needed to grocery shop and pick up the dry-cleaning and get the car washed all in one day. It wasn't because they had to do their hair and nails and pick out an outfit for a big event. It wasn't because their apartment wasn't getting cleaned or the meals weren't getting prepped.

Jesus preached a message of rest because His people were being sent out into communities to preach the truth, perform miracles, heal people, and more. They were traveling all around the known world to tell everybody they could about the hope they had found. They were getting close to the ostracized and forgotten. They were spending time with the sick and the lame. They were healing the people society had rejected. They were getting up early and walking for miles on dusty roads and investing in people and crossing divides and fighting for change.

And on top of it all, they were being terrorized, abused, and persecuted for all the goodness they were trying to do. In fact, Jesus warned them earlier,

"Stay alert. This is hazardous work I'm assigning you. You're going to be like sheep running through a wolf pack, so don't call attention to yourselves. Be as shrewd as a snake, inoffensive as a dove.

> Don't be naive. Some people will question your motives, others will smear your reputation—just because you believe in me. Don't be upset when they haul you before the civil authorities."

MATTHEW 10:16-18, MSG

These people were being run out of town and brought before the authorities, all while their motives and reputations were dragged through the dirt. They were pouring themselves out for the sake of Christ. They were sacrificing everything to do the work of Jesus.

When I read this passage, I can't help but picture the meeting Jesus had with His disciples once they returned home from their first expedition. I imagine Jesus waiting under a tree, leaning up against the trunk as He watches each of the disciples trickle back into town. I can see Him waving them over as they collapse onto the dust beneath the shade of the branches. It's quiet. No one is speaking. They're too tired to speak, too sore from days of walking to stay standing, too exhausted even to think about finding a meal. They're wiping the sweat off their dust-creased foreheads and trying not to sit in a way that reminds them of the bruises they received as they were pushed out of town. They rest their heads on their knees, trying to block out the yelling that still rings in their ears, the shouts and accusations. Tears hang in their eyes as they sit with the discouragement of days full of failure after failure after failure.

Maybe they're ready to throw it all away. Maybe they're done. Rejection, hate, persecution, discouragement, and weariness certainly isn't what they signed up for . . . right?

And it's in *this* moment, as He looks at this ragtag group of discouraged twentysomethings, I imagine Jesus smiling gently and saying, "Now, it's time to rest."

He created a Sabbath and even modeled for us what it looks like to rest from work that matters. Sometimes we look around and say to an overly rested, apathetic culture, "Just rest. Jesus said it was important." But we never seem to clarify *why* Jesus would tell His followers to take this deep, soulful rest in the first place.

We never seem to ask the question: What are we actually resting *from*?

Don't stop doing the things that really matter. The things you were created to do. The things Jesus designed for you to pour your life into. Keep going. You are not on this earth to discover the perfect balance or routine or rhythm. The greatest commandment is not, "Rest, even if it means your life becomes entirely focused on yourself. Get another manicure, watch one more episode, do some more shopping, make sure your meals are prepped."

The greatest commandments are

1. love God; and
2. love people.

So, let's rest in preparation for the ways we have been called to love God and love people. Let's rest *after* pouring ourselves out for the sake of Jesus and His hope spreading through the world. Let's rest *to prepare* to affect more eternities, fight for more lasting justice, and spread true hope into our culture.

And while we are allowing Jesus to fill us with Himself, let's ask ourselves honestly, *What am I resting* from? *And is it worthy of my one and only life?*

There are some things in your life that are really good and right. The things you were born to do. The wrongs you were born to make right. The passions God has placed deep within your soul. Don't stop those things. Because they are exactly what makes your life feel full and beautiful and risky and adventurous in all of the right ways.

Keep going.

Keep going to the part of town with a large homeless population and creating relationships there.

Keep going to basketball games to cheer on the young men and women you mentor.

Keep serving at your church.

Keep running races to raise money for the causes you believe in.

Keep investing in the lives of younger leaders around you.

Keep inviting people into your life.

Keep creating relationships with the families of refugees in your community.

Keep taking foster children into your home.

Keep advocating for the rights of the oppressed.

Keep reaching across lines of division and fighting for peace.

Keep befriending people who don't know Jesus.

Keep standing up for the foreigner.

Keep investing in the life of the high schooler who is wondering if her life is still worth living.

This is what you were created to do.

And keep painting.

Keep singing.

Keep dancing.

Keep writing.

Keep creating.

Keep taking pictures.

Keep exploring.

Keep building.

Keep dreaming.

This is what makes your soul come alive. And we need your soul to be alive.

Keep loving your family faithfully.
Keep showing up for your friends.
Keep creating deep, authentic relationships.
Keep crafting real community.
This is what it feels like to be human.
Friends—let's keep going.

THE ANTHEM OF A LIFE THAT MATTERS

"Honestly, I'm surprised you showed up. My buddies didn't expect two girls from Chicago to actually rock climb in this weather," our guide told us as we began to put on our gear. I laughed. Clearly his buddies didn't know how stubborn two girls from Chicago could be.

It was shaping up to be a dreamy day. The kind of day that is almost as magical to remember as it is to live. My friend and I were spending the week in one of the most captivating corners of our country—the Pacific Northwest.

While we were there, my friend gave me the best surprise. I hopped in the car without a clue of where we were going. "For your birthday," my friend began, "we have a private guide taking us rock climbing in the gorges right outside of Portland."

She filmed my reaction, and let's just say my

friends mocked my celebration for months. It was April in Oregon, which means it was cool and wet and overcast and breezy. Not exactly the ideal conditions for rock climbing. But we were committed to embrace every soggy moment.

We gingerly traversed the bright-green, mossy terrain. Our eyes feasted on the bubbling brooks and gentle waterfalls and multicolored rocks as we made our way toward our first climb. Suddenly, our guide threw his well-worn rope bag onto the ground, causing the mud to splash our ankles. "This is it. Let's get started."

My excitement grew as my gaze slowly drifted up the rock. The mix of adrenaline and cold shivers running up and down my spine had officially erased any possibility of fear in my mind. I was giddy with excitement, tying my figure-eight knot as my hands shook with anticipation.

The climb was everything I had hoped it would be. Every deep breath, every big reach, every carefully placed foot led me higher and higher. I tried hard to mark every single moment and remember each beautiful view. I think God loves when we discover the things in His world that cause our hearts to beat faster and come alive.

If you're a painter, I think God loves when you paint. If you're a poet, I think God loves when you write. If you're a runner, I think God loves when you run. If you're a musician, I think God loves when you play. If you're a climber, I think God loves when you climb. If you're an explorer, I think God loves when you explore. If you're a parent, I think God loves when you hold your children close. If you're a leader, I think God loves when you lead. If you're a builder, I think God loves when you craft things with your hands.

I think God loves to watch His children's hearts come alive. And mine comes alive when I climb.

Eventually, we sat down on a large, smooth gray rock to catch our breath. As we sat, immersed in the magic of the bright-green foliage and the hazy-blue mist and the sunrays streaming through the tree branches, the silence hung heavy. It felt as though if we spoke, we'd disrupt the sacred moment and the beauty around us would melt away.

Then, gently, the deep, sage voice of our guide broke the seal of silence. He began to weave together stories that captured our attention, made our eyes open wide with wonder, and filled the space around us with narratives of climbing. He spoke of the wild, passionate souls who had come before us. He told the stories of the women and men who spent hours and hours with hammers in hand, pounding the bolts into the hard rock face to create a path for others. It wasn't an easy job. They poured out their time and their sweat and their blood.

Creating this path demanded deep levels of

sacrifice. But for these passionate climbers, it was worth it. They understood they weren't just building routes for themselves—they were blazing trails for many others to come. Our guide's eyes rested on the rock face before us as though he could still see those rugged trailblazers building, working, pounding, creating.

Suddenly, he looked back at us and said, "You know, if it wasn't for those climbers, you would have no idea how to climb to the top of this wall."

At first, I was offended. My stubborn spirit flared, and my independent streak flashed. I wanted to tell him I could have created my own path, forged my own trail, found my own way up to the top. But as the flare fizzled and the flash faded, I realized he was right.

Without those bolts, we would have been left to fend for ourselves. We would have been searching for a path. We would have been groping for a route. We wouldn't have had a secure place to clip our ropes. We would have wandered off course. We would have been left on our own.

But. Someone had chosen to do the hard work, to go before us, to make the sacrifices and to pound the bolts into the walls. And because of them, I knew exactly how to journey from where I was to where I wanted to be. I could climb with confidence. I could set out with certainty. The path was blazed. All I had to do was start climbing.

And in the sacredness of that moment, something clicked.

We, in this moment, are the ones who must put on our gear, grab our hammers, and pound some bolts into the walls of this world. It's time for us to blaze a trail into a whole new way of living. It's time to boldly step out to create a path for future generations.

It starts with us.

As we begin to live lives that really matter, lives so full of beauty and passion and risk and impact that we practically leak change everywhere we go, we'll catch the attention of a world hungry, yearning, searching for meaning, for purpose, for fulfillment, for adventure. And when we do, we'll trace it all back to the very Revolutionary who taught us what living a life that matters looks like. Jesus Christ will be seen for who He really is: a dynamic leader whose selfless love drove Him to a cross for me and for you.

When we really know Jesus, we can't help but want to spend our entire lives following Him and telling everyone about this God who demonstrates a wildly unprecedented kind of love. We really can't.

He was a rebel with a cause worth fighting for. He was a revolutionary whose followers shook up the world. He was a pioneer who turned the religious system upside down. He was a leader whose life and death and resurrection changed everything for everyone.

He offended the religious. He shocked the influential.

He challenged the wealthy. He questioned the royalty. He shook up the order of the world that everyone else had accepted as normal.

And instead, He hung out with the rejects. He spent time with the prostitutes. He cared for the infected and homeless and needy. He gave leadership roles to the young outcasts. He empowered women to lead in His church. He boasted this wildly unprecedented, different brand of love.

We are not rallying around a political cause, or a religion, or a brand, or an idea, or a belief system, or a list of rules, or even a church. We are rallying around the person of Jesus Christ and the movement He started over two thousand years ago with His team of wild, brave teens and twentysomethings.

I could try to describe who Jesus is. But I couldn't ever dream of saying it as beautifully or poetically as the Bible says it. I just can't help but point us to the Bible. Not because I *have to* like the Bible if I claim to follow Jesus. But because I simply have never read any more beautiful, hope-filled, love-centered words in my entire life. It is not just a book we read at church. It's a vision for a whole new kind of world. It's the rallying cry for an unprecedented kind of love. It puts words to the deepest whispers of my soul and yearnings of my heart. So come with me into this beautiful jungle of words written by the very revolutionaries who started this movement in the first place.

He is a Jesus who says,

"I created you to be free people, abundantly free people. So don't let the world, which doesn't know the first thing about living, tell you how to live. Because you were made alive in me. And in me you find out who you are and what you're living for. You're no longer wandering exiles. I'm using you. I can do far more in your life and through your life than you could ever imagine or guess or request in your wildest dreams. Take in the extravagant dimensions of my love. Come follow me and I will show you how to live full lives, full in my fullness."

AUTHOR'S PARAPHRASE OF EPHESIANS 1:7-14; 2:19-22, MSG

This Jesus has captured my soul. He is the One I want to give my everything to. The One I want everyone to know about. The One I want to know more and more and more of. And, more than anything else, I want to live like Him.

He looks us in the eyes and says, "If you really want to live a full life, just come with me. I can show you how. I can show you what that means. I created you to live life to the *full*, and I want to see you live it. Just come with me. But get ready, because it's going to be a wild ride. I'll show you how to live a life that matters."

The invitation isn't "Come to church." The invitation was never "Come, follow My rules." The invitation is not "Settle for a life that is empty and safe and regulated."

Here is what we are invited to:

God's Spirit beckons. There are things to do and places to go!

This resurrection life you received from God is not a timid, grave-tending life. It's adventurously expectant, greeting God with a childlike "What's next, Papa?"

ROMANS 8:14-15, MSG

Our world is searching for an adventurously expectant life. And instead, people often find themselves experiencing something that feels more like a grave-tending life. Because Jesus is the only way we can truly begin to live a life that matters.

Jesus isn't searching for somebody else—because He already selected you.

A fresh wind is about to be unleashed in our world. A wind of young leaders refusing to live an average existence. A wind of historymakers discovering a cause worthy of their passion. A wind of world changers battling against injustice. A wind of trailblazers fighting to become a truly distinct generation.

It doesn't matter how young you are or how unqualified you feel. You are invited to be a part of this tribe.

"JESUS ISN'T SEARCHING FOR
SOMEBODY ELSE—BECAUSE HE
ALREADY SELECTED YOU."

Let's abandon the apathy and the mediocrity. Let's refuse to wait until a better season or a more convenient time comes along. Let's stop disqualifying ourselves and believing the lies of this world.

Instead, let's claim the potential we have through the power of Jesus Christ.

Let's craft our passion and discover the wrongs we were born to make right.

Let's find our people and link arms in unity.

And together, let's live lives that truly matter.

THE CHARGE

I had no idea that history was being made.
I was just tired of giving up.
ROSA PARKS

I WISH I COULD TELL YOU I've discovered all the secrets of this magical, beautiful, new kind of life. But I haven't. And I'm okay with that. Because even this life, the kind that really matters, doesn't always feel perfect. In fact, it often feels messy and hard and exhausting. And, in some ways, that's the point. Because our lives aren't about achieving some level of perfection. They're so much richer than that.

Whenever I come to the end of a meaningful book I'm reading, I always wonder, *What's next?* While I am reading the book, I am convinced my life will never be the same. I'm sure I'll change, I'll live differently, and I'll *be* different. But then I close the book, set it on the shelf, and go back to my life.

In the wake of a life-giving challenge, everything usually goes back to normal. Our schedules don't change. Our routines stay the same. Our priorities are exactly what they were before we started reading.

And you can do that after you finish this book too. You can stay the same.

You *can*. But you're bolder than that. You're braver. You're wilder. You're riskier.

You are the kind of person who has what it takes to live a life that matters.

You are a soul who has a story worth telling.

You are a revolutionary with a wrong you were born to make right.

You are a leader who could shake up the world.

You are an influencer who could usher justice into your community.

You are an activist who could create sustainable change in our world.

You are a unifier who could bring our world together.

You are a trailblazer who could build a better future.

You are the one, and now is the time.

Don't waste one more day, one more hour, one more moment living a story you were never created to write. Let's do something different.

There is a world waiting to be changed, and you have everything you need to change it. There are women praying to be rescued from their exploiters. There are children praying for someone to invite them into a family. There are refugees praying for someone to welcome them. There are fathers praying to find food for their children. There are high schoolers praying for someone to care about their lives. There are families praying for a roof over their heads. There are girls praying for a chance at an education. There are villages praying for clean water to reach them.

And *we* are God's answer. *We* are the answer to the world's greatest needs.

We're together on this journey. When we're exhausted; when we're angry; when we're burdened; when it all just feels too heavy; when we're in the mess of injustice, the trials of challenge, the beauty of love, the pain of sacrifice, the hope of unity, the wildness of risk, the fierceness of the fight—remember, we're doing this side by side. And if we persevere, the world will never be the same.

So let's link arms and proclaim our commitment to stay in this fight:

We may be tired, but we won't quit.

We may be beaten down, but we won't retreat.

We may be discouraged, but we won't give up.

We may be counted out, but we won't believe the lies.

We may be told to quit, but we won't stop.

We may be unqualified, but we won't make excuses.

We may be afraid, but we won't run away.

We'll step up, show up, stay in the fight.

We'll raise our voice and rally for change and refuse to stay the same.

We'll abandon the mediocre and live lives of meaning.

We'll leave behind our comfort and step forward into courage.

We'll rescue the marginalized and empower the oppressed.

We'll remember the forgotten and give a voice to the silenced.

We'll reach across divides and link arms with those who are different.

We'll sacrifice and surrender and stay, even when it's hard.

We'll write stories of wild, unprecedented kinds of love.

We'll build a better future for the generations to come.

This is the anthem. This is our anthem.

This is the anthem of Generation Distinct.

THIS IS NOT A BOOK END.
IN FACT, YOUR STORY IS JUST GETTING STARTED.

Take action and begin your journey of discovering the wrong you were uniquely born to make right by going to generationdistinct.com/yournextstep.

HOW DOES IT WORK?

Each step of *Generation Distinct's* Four Step Journey is an online tool you can complete from anywhere in the world created with YOU in mind.

STEP #1: OWN YOUR POTENTIAL

Engage in this twelve-session video series, where you will have the opportunity to discover what is really happening in our world from experts who are in the fight against some of the most prevalent injustices in our world. Then you'll be equipped with the next steps you need to take action in the fight against these injustices.

STEP #2: CRAFT YOUR PASSION

Enter into a four-month experience to craft your own custom World Change Strategy. In this program, you will spend two months discovering the wrong you were born to make right and two months being trained on that passion, all alongside your own personal leadership guide.

STEP #3: FIND YOUR PEOPLE

Be welcomed into a coalition of radical world changers from around the globe who will link arms with you to live the distinct life.

STEP #4: LIVE DISTINCT

Receive direct mentorship, compelling next steps, unique opportunities, incredible connections, and invitations to exclusive trips and events all designed to unleash you to live the distinct life right where you are.

ACKNOWLEDGMENTS

IF YOU ASKED ME AS A LITTLE GIRL what I wanted to be when I grew up, I would have told you a writer—to use words and stories to reach people and inspire others and create change. That dream is a reality today because of the *many* people who have lived this story with me.

Here's just a little glimpse of who those people are. Thank you to . . .

My parents. You have always believed in the dreams God has given me. You are my unfair advantage in this life. Thank you for the hours you spent reading my many stories and poems growing up. I am forever grateful and proud to be your daughter.

Jul, Josh, and Todd. Thanks for believing in the voice of your sister. Thanks for always keeping me grounded. I am who I am today because of you.

Faith. The dreams we dreamed on the porch swing are happening. Can you believe it? I am forever grateful for our decades of sisterhood. You are one of the boldest, wisest leaders I have ever met.

Sarah. Thanks for taking me rock climbing in Oregon. You celebrate people so well. That day was an adventure I will never, ever forget. I am so grateful for your friendship.

Alex Bryjak. So much love for being a part of so many important moments of my life. Since day one of GenD, you have been there. Thanks for taking my first speaking photos all the way to the photo for this book.

Thank you to the many friends, my TRIBE, who have supported this vision in countless ways. You know who you are. You have believed in this project, breathed life into my vision, cheered me on when I was discouraged, and linked arms with me in this wild adventure of life.

Aubrey Sampson. Your mentorship has changed my life. Thank you for the hours you spent with me sitting at your kitchen table, helping me prepare the book proposal. You and Kevin have loved me, shown up for me, and invested in me in more ways than I could ever name.

So much gratitude to Danielle Strickland. Thank you for inviting me into your life, calling out greatness in me, empowering me to lead, and believing in my voice. I'm glad we survived our ride in my Jeep. Forever grateful for your presence and influence in my life.

Nicole Defalco. You have become one of the most

important voices in my life. Thank you for teaching me business and entrepreneurship and what it looks like to be a powerful woman who leads with great humility.

The Generation Distinct board. Your wisdom, brilliance, and belief in this vision have always blown me away. GenD is what it is today because of *you*.

Thanks to the Generation Team, both past and present. I truly love you people. You all inspire me. You are bold, brilliant, and passionate world changers, and I consider it one of the greatest honors of my life to link arms with you as we chase after this vision together.

Thank you to Don Gates, Don Pape, Caitlyn Carlson, Robin Bermel, Olivia Eldredge, and Mark Lane for being such an essential part of making this book a reality. I'm forever grateful. You saw the potential in this project and believed in this vision. I cannot believe I was gifted the opportunity to work with each one of you.

And finally, thank you to the man who fans the flame of my calling every day. Aaron Barnett—the way you live and lead inspires me to live an even more distinct life. Thank you for being *with* me in the exciting public moments *and* in the ordinary everyday moments. I am more fully the woman God has created me to be with you in my life. I didn't know you when I wrote this book, but now I can't imagine my life without you. #TeamDream

GENERATION DISTINCT MOVEMENTS

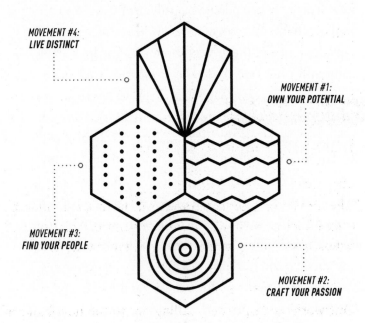

MOVEMENT #4:
LIVE DISTINCT

MOVEMENT #1:
OWN YOUR POTENTIAL

MOVEMENT #3:
FIND YOUR PEOPLE

MOVEMENT #2:
CRAFT YOUR PASSION

INDEX OF SHAREABLE STATEMENTS

MOVEMENT #1

"I really want to live a life that matters."

"The most monumental moments of history can often be traced back to a small, passionate band of brothers and sisters who refused to allow the world to stay as it was."

"Our world is desperately calling out to the next band of passionate, gritty, tenacious young leaders, asking them to rise up and demand a different type of world."

"The question isn't *whether* the world will be changed. The question is, who will change it?"

"What injustice could be crossed off because your name comes onto the scene?"

"You have an essential, pivotal role in God's strategy for the redemption and restoration of this world."

"You're *invited* into this wild adventure of life."

"Let's link arms together as we storm the gates of this world with truth and love and honor and justice and light."

"Our world is ready to realize a radical new way to live."

"The future generations depend on us to break the chains and blaze the trail."

"The opposite of monotony is not excitement. The opposite of monotony is meaning."

"We have something to learn from the most influential person in all of history."

"What if our generation could be the answer to the world's greatest needs?"

"When we are pushed out of what's comfortable, to the edge of where we think we can go, suddenly we discover how God equips us to go even further."

"We can be the people who dare to defy all the old, rigid rules."

"This season of our lives as young leaders isn't just preparation for our lives. This *is* our lives."

"You have the potential to live a life that matters."

MOVEMENT #2

"You will never regret choosing the path you were born to live."

"Welcome is not just something you extend to people

who look like you, or talk like you, or come from the same background as you. It's for everyone."

"Unity only arrives when we abdicate our advantage."

"I don't think it's wrong if we doubt God. I do think it's wrong if we allow that doubt to prevent us from exploring the depths of God."

"When we show unprecedented kinds of love, we change the narrative of our world."

"This is the moment when we decide a more beautiful world is still possible, and we are going to be part of fighting for it."

"We become so consumed with *discovering* our passion that we never actually *do* anything about the injustice invading our world."

"We're just waiting because it's easier to use our lack of clarity as an excuse rather than actually doing something."

"There is a wrong you were born to make right."

"It's time to do *something*."

"There is so much exciting and beautiful work to be done. God is inviting us to be a part of what He is doing in the world."

"Sustaining our passion is more difficult than making the decision to pursue a new passion."

"We love them through our consistency."

"We don't get to dictate when or how God speaks. He just speaks."

"Refuse to back down, to quit, or to retreat. Stay on the front lines of this fight."

"I think the suffering and the beauty can all be rolled into one significant life."

"If we follow the One whose beautiful life of purpose led Him to a cross, we must be prepared for deep sacrifice and real cost."

"God wants to equip you with everything you need to make wrongs right, in every paradoxical part of it."

MOVEMENT #3

"If we are the heroes of our own story, we get to engage in justice when it makes us look good."

"When we turn people into *others*, we begin to believe that justice is about occasionally helping people who are different and then retreating back into our cozy, middle-class churches, as we pat ourselves on the back for being the heroes."

"Jesus walked the earth, He heard our stories, He touched our pain, and He embraced our messy lives. . . . He lived and died alongside real people, and, as He did, He ushered true and lasting justice into their lives."

"Jesus came to give Himself away, not to be the hero. And He created you to give yourself away, not to be the hero."

"No matter our ethnicity or our income level, our gender or our nationality, our immigration status or whether we have a place to call home—Jesus just sees people. Do we?"

"We won't bring any lasting, real, sustainable, systemic change if our entire aim is a singular heroic life."

"The fight against injustice in our world isn't a walk-in-the-park kind of fight. This is an all-out, give-everything-you-have, make-deep-sacrifices, get-right-in-the-mess, fall-down-and-get-up kind of fight. And if we're in it for ourselves, we just won't last."

"Our fight for justice must always come from a deep, holy, radical, dangerous kind of love."

"We are *not* the heroes. We are something better: We are love. And love actually changes things."

"Sometimes we have to create the things we long to be a part of."

"That's what it means to build unity. It means we honor the image of God that lies within every single person."

"I don't think our world is full of tension and conflict and disunity because we really hate each other. I think we just don't know each other. And I think we're afraid of what we don't know."

"If we ever want to witness our world come together in unity, we must build communities of God's wildly diverse people."

"What if our tribes were a mosaic of lives, stories, perspectives, backgrounds, opinions, ideas, and cultures?"

"We all benefit when we choose to invite more voices to the table."

"We are better when we are united. We are stronger when we are diverse. We are bolder when we link arms."

"The souls of humanity call out for people."

"The opportunity to do life within a group of people who are unafraid to be with you and for you and go deep is one of the most beautiful, sacred gifts God has given to us."

"It is not someone else's responsibility to fill the cravings of our own souls."

"It is *our* responsibility to do the things that set our souls on fire."

"Take whatever you love and combine it with your love for Jesus; then invite some people to join you to create real change in the world."

"Even the Son of God knew there was value in doing life, changing the world, and starting a movement alongside a tribe of people."

"The tribe you have been searching for, yearning for, and desperately seeking after could very well be on the other side of your step of bravery."

"You were created for a tribe. So go out and create your own."

"We were never designed to do great work in this world on our own. We were formed for unity. We were created to link arms. We were handcrafted with a longing to belong."

"Life is so much more magical and meaningful when you are surrounded by a tribe of people who are characterized by all the crazy and wildest kinds of love."

MOVEMENT #4

"We don't need more money or time or permission. We just need to say yes. It's up to us."

"We don't have to know the whole story when we begin writing the first chapter."

"Our generation is at risk of missing writing the big story altogether because we're so worried we'll start the first chapter wrong."

"Life is happening right now all around us, in all of its intoxicating beauty and whimsy and unpredictability. So let's just do the thing. Let's build the lives we want to live. Let's mold existences we fall in love with over and over and over. Let's write stories we love to read."

"Your life is not happening to you. You are happening to your life."

"So many of us are living like the greatest call on our life is self-preservation, so we don't put ourselves in positions to feel afraid, or unsure, or uncomfortable, or stretched, or exhausted, or embarrassed, or in over our heads."

"Every single one of my heroes has built a life centered on the very things we run so far away from."

"Jesus isn't searching for somebody else—because He already selected you."

"*We* are the answer to the world's greatest needs."

NOTES

FOREWORD
1. G. K. Chesterton, "What's Wrong with the World" in *The Collected Works of G. K. Chesterton* vol. 4 (San Francisco: Ignatius Press, 1987), 61.

MOVEMENT #2 CRAFT YOUR PASSION
1. See Matthew 2:13-14.
2. William Wilberforce, "On the Horrors of the Slave Trade," from a speech in the House of Commons (May 12, 1789).

MOVEMENT #4 LIVE DISTINCT
1. See Jeremiah 22 and James 1:27.